".....Never As It Seems!"

A look at television news from the other side of the screen

by
Bill Brubaker

Published by

PEANUT BUTTER
PUBLISHING

Seattle, WA

Published by
Peanut Butter Publishing
200 Second Avenue West
Seattle, WA 98119
(206) 281-5965
Printed in Canada

Contents

Introduction

Broadcasting, like other industries, has evolved over the years. In the pioneering era of broadcasting, men like Bill Dubillier, Vince Kraft and Louis Wasmer "tinkered" their way into the Broadcasting Hall of Fame. Dubillier did it in 1910. He was convinced that if one could send sound over a wire like Morse's telegraph, then there might be a way to transmit the human voice. By taking power from the third rail of the trolley that ran between Auburn and Kent Dubillier managed to modulate the wires in the light bulbs. Imagine the surprise of trolley passengers when they heard music coming from the light fixtures. Vincent Kraft confined his tinkering to the garage of his University District home and by 1921 KJR was

---

[1] A "spoonerism" is the inadvertant transposition of letters. This is a spoonerism of the Nooksack Valley of Washington State.

almost a household word. Louis Wasmer built KHQ in Seattle, loaded the parts aboard a motorcycle sidecar and went to Spokane. That was 1926.

From the late thirties to the fifties was radio's "Golden Age" when the Masked Rider of the Plains and his faithful Indian companion compelled us to drop everything and gather around the Philco each afternoon at five. Orson Welles convinced us the Martians were coming and there was always "good news tonight!" from Gabriel Heatter.

When television came on the scene many of our heroes and heroines found that it was just as profitable to be seen as well as heard, and the radio industry found itself looking for something to do. As for television? What can one say? It has, as Erik Barnouw characterized in his 1975 book, become a *Tube of Plenty*.

Today all one has to do is stop, look and listen to know that radio found plenty to do despite the fact that television has become as much a part of our lives as eating and sleeping. Radio gave up its serials, soaps and mystery playhouses to become a background medium of music, talk and weather reports. Full studio orchestras gave way to records and compact disks and the "Voice of Firestone" became a disc jockey.

Radio had already transitioned to its present form by the time I began my career in the late fifties. After stints as an announcer, rock 'n' roll disk jockey and radio newsman, I was overcome by the lure of a more lucrative career in television news.

It must be human nature to think that "your" time was the best time and that which followed could never quite measure up. But as I look at television news today I see an industry in love with itself, no longer content with "telling it as it is." Today each story is embellished with electronic accessories to make it "sell." The newscasters themselves are color-coded, washed, and pressed. And the intense competition for viewers has resulted in a tabloid mentality that puts into our living rooms stories that until now were confined to the supermarket check-out stands. Television news relies too much on technology and not enough on the skill and energy of people.

It is easy to see why, human nature notwithstanding, I think my time was the best time.

This book is not about technology, nor is it about the rules of journalistic assembly. It is about wonderful people, skilled and energetic people who weren't afraid to make mistakes along the way or share a wart or two with the audience. It's about people who measured humor as important as integrity and discovered it wasn't so bad to laugh at oneself.

In the following pages I seek not to ridicule nor put down, but to share with you the people and events that made "my" time the best time...and to illustrate that broadcast news, now and then is...**Never As It Seems!**

Bill Brubaker, 1992

"That George Shearing is outta sight!"[2]

Sandy Hill,
KIRO-TV
Seattle, Washington

Acknowledgements

I am grateful to a great many people for their help and encouragement in writing this book. Some of them include Elliott Wolf whose frequent admonishment to "stay well" was for his own success as well as my own...Brian Herbert, who, along with his red pencil, gave a literary touch to this work...Heather Hitson, for her artistic skills...Sharon Dale, without whom nobody would know what Elliott, Brian, Heather and I had done...Jennifer Johnson, for her scheduling expertise...my wife Marlene who, by laughing in all the right places, encouraged me...the hundreds of colleagues who gave substance to the memories, some of which are written here...and KOMO which continues to make me feel as welcome now as when I worked there.

---

[2] George Shearing was a blind piano player.

KOMO-TV's W.W. Warren (center) in the early 1950s as station manager. He and KOMO-TV Engineer Stan Bennett show off the latest black and white television camera.

"Don't tell me about
a busted forecast, I just
shoveled four inches
of partly cloudy off
my driveway!"

Bill Brubaker, KOMO-TV
Seattle, Washington

Dedication

To W. W.

Very often it's nice to be recognized, but I have
never been so wrapped up in what I do for a living that
I feel a need to make sure everyone knows me.

There were dozens of times when I was called
Bruce. I had no problem with that. After all, it does
sound a lot like Bill. And Dave, well, I'm sure a certain jazz musician would have been flattered. Most of
the time they had the right television station and that
was good enough for me.

Where you would never expect that to happen,
however, was in your own broadcasting company.
After, all fifteen years working under the same roof
should give one an edge in being known, especially by
the Chief Executive Officer. W.W. Warren had as-
cended to the top spot through hard work. Despite the
fact his uncle, O.D. Fisher, owned the place, W.W.
learned everything there was to learn about the business by working his way up through the ranks. He was
a no-nonsense businessman who believed one could
make money and serve the public at the same time,
and that the most important product he had to offer
was the employees he represented.

One day while walking through the station on an errand, I stopped by Art McDonald's office where he was holding forth with the CEO.

"Hi Mister Warren," I said, rather loudly, because W.W. was slightly hard of hearing. He turned, smiled and said, "Hello, Bob!"

Hello, Bob? Geeez, I suddenly had the urge to grab him by the lapels and look him in his two good eyes and shout into his one good ear..."It's Bill, not Bob! Read my lips...its B-I-L-L!" I did say, didn't I, that this sort of thing didn't usually bother me? Just the night before, however, the weatherman had called me "Bob" on the air, and several days before that one of our field reporters said after his report..."Back to you, Bob!" So when the BOSS called me "Bob," well, that was the last straw. I had, it seemed, only three choices: correct him...forget it...or change my name to Bob. Forgetting it seemed easiest.

It would have been nice if Art and a few others on the staff would have forgotten it. Fat chance. Come on, guys, it was a natural mistake and anyway, how was W.W. to know that I had been called "Bob" twice that week already? But the next morning when I came into my office there was on my desk the photograph of W.W. Warren that usually hangs in the lobby. Taped to it was a piece of paper in the shape of one of those cartoon balloons upon which was written the words "Hi Bob!"

So this is how it's going to be, I thought. It was funny and, of course, the whole news room was waiting for me to show up and see the photograph. We all had a good laugh. For the next several weeks whenever I ventured around the station, it was the same...."Hi, Bob.....Howya doin', Bob?....Why it's Bob Brubaker....Hey Bob"...and so on, *ad nauseam*.

Now you know that sooner or later Mr. Warren was going to hear about this, since at times communication in the communication business could be incredible. He did hear about it, including an offhand remark I made that the next time I saw him I was going to say..."Mister WARNER."

The measure of a man, I believe, is the ability to laugh at himself in the midst of great responsibility. A sense of humor is a wonderful thing, and several days after the "Hello, Bob" incident, I received this note from the BOSS:

Fisher Broadcasting Inc.

KOMO Radio and Television, KATU Television, ABC Affiliates.

W. W. Warren
President and Chief Executive Officer

Dear ~~Bob~~ Bill ~

It just got around to me. I apologize!

— Bill ~~Warner~~

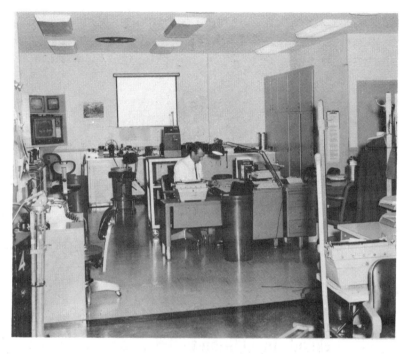

*Author Bill Brubaker in the 1965 KOMO-TV Newsroom. It
was a lonely job in those days but somebody had to do it.
(Note the absence of electronic devices.)*

CHAPTER 1

"Pardon Me, But Your Pink Slip is Showing!"

For many of us our first broadcast jobs were in radio. It was a logical rung on the ladder of success, and besides, in those days there weren't a lot of television jobs to go around. While there is little doubt they were the best of times, they were also times when I came close to getting my walking papers.

I was hired as a radio news reporter and, being at the bottom of the seniority totem, was assigned to work weekends in addition to three days during the week. I didn't have a family then, so the schedule wasn't so bad. Frankly I found it a welcome respit from the weekday grind of news gathering.

It was 1962, and the Seattle World's Fair was underway. With the station just across the street from the fairgrounds, people were always wandering into the studio. Most of them just wanted to look around a little, use the restrooms and leave. Some wanted full tours of the station. We were instructed to be diligent and discourage those without business, asking them to hold their curiosity and bladders in check until a weekday when there was sufficient staff to take care of them.

I had been at the station for only a couple of weeks. It was Saturday and I was working the dayshift. Just me, a teletype, the announcer, a 100 pound switchboard operator and a whole lot of time. I had just completed a radio broadcast and walked back into the news room from the studio. The phone rang.

"News room," I answered.

It was the switchboard operator.

"Can you please come out here?" she asked. I heard urgency in her voice....an urgency that told this highly perceptive news person she needed help.

"Be right there," I said, and hung up. I had no idea why she needed help. All sorts of things went through my mind, including an incident at another station in another town where a disgruntled fan had driven his car through the front doors of the station and plowed into the telephone operator's station. I knew that wasn't the case this time...at least I hadn't heard a crash.

"What's the problem?" I asked as I reached the lobby.

"That!" she said and pointed down the hall. Walking away, his back toward us, was an elderly fellow, dressed in painter's overalls and a painter's cap, both looking as if they had never been washed.

"Who's he?" I asked.

"I dunno. He just came in the door as if he owned the place....looked at me and before I could say anything was off wandering down the hall."

"I'll take care of it," I said in my best radio newsman's voice. "Leave it to me!"

I bolted down the hall after the man. He was a kindly-looking fellow, in his seventies, I would guess, and he kind of shuffled as he walked. Reaching him in a few strides, I gently grasped him by the arm, turned him around and headed back up the hall to the lobby and the front door. As we walked I explained, in a firm but kindly voice, that the station wasn't open during the weekends and we couldn't let anyone just walk in off the street and walk about as he or she pleased. Frankly, I said, I was too busy to take him around, and I explained further that if he really wanted to see the station he could come by or call Monday for an appointment.

Timing is everything. I finished my speech just as we reached the door and with a pleasant goodbye, nudged him onto the street.

As I turned to walk back into the lobby, the switchboard operator gave me one of those "Gee, you're wonderful" looks. I retired to the news room feeling very satisfied with my first effort at corporate assertiveness.

The following Monday I reported for work early in the morning, as usual. About ten I got a call from the station's program director. He wanted to see me in his office. Oh boy, I thought to myself, here it comes...a reward, a pat on the back, the undying gratitude of the "higher-ups" for protecting the station from the old man in overalls. What a deal, I thought, here only a couple of weeks and I was already making points.

Once in the "PD's" office, I sat down, anxiously awaiting the accolades that were about to come.

"You remember that old man who came in here Saturday, like he owned the place?" the Program Director asked.

"I sure do!" I replied.

"Well," the PD said, "His name is Fisher and he does!"

Cap'n Puget (Don McCune) and Salty (Freddy Lloyd) with their pal, the irascible "Barney."

CHAPTER 2

"Polly Want a Job?"

The only other time I came close to getting my walking papers occurred several years later. I had, in fact, resigned from KOMO Radio to pursue an advanced degree at the University of Washington. So that I might support my family and school, I applied for a job in the production department of KOMO Television. I was hired as a "floor director," a euphemism for "stage hand." Despite my initial disdain for the job, which lasted just a year, it was more fun per hour than any job before or since. That's not to say it was all play and no work. It was mostly work, but there seemed to be more opportunities for relieving the pressures of work.

In its simplest form, the job involved building sets, taking them down, cleaning up, making sure the water glass was filled with water and whatever else the talent liked. The floor director was also an extension of the director—cueing talent and holding cue cards. Usually there were two floor directors for each show. My partner in mischief was former Marine and ex-Husky Rose-Bowler Forrest "Tim" Bullard who would later host a very successful sports program and eventually became a member of the KOMO-TV Sales Department. Tim and I hit it off from the start, probably because we were kindred spirits when it came to a good joke...even on each other!

One of the "live" shows on which we worked was the Captain Puget Show starring Don McCune as Cap'n Puget, Freddy Lloyd as "Salty" and Barney as....Barney. Barney was a parrot. You see, in those days in order to have a successful children's program, one had to have an animal. Bill McLean over at Channel 11 had Crazy Donkey, Stan Boreson at KING-TV had NOMO the Under-Achiever Bassett Hound, and over at Channel 7, JP Patches had the next best thing to an animal, Ketchikan the Animal Man. All of them, it seemed, had some redeeming value. Not Barney. Barney was the crummiest looking, most ill-tempered parrot that ever lived.

Despite his animal-like behavior, Barney was part and parcel of the Cap'n Puget Show. He was always there, sitting atop a rusty diver's helmet that served as his perch. He just sat there, turned around a couple of times a show, squawked once in a while, and that was it. In the years I knew that dumb bird, he never, ever said a word. Not a peep!

Well, he did, once!

Over coffee one day Tim and I decided it was time that Barney learned how to talk. And who better to teach him than a couple of college-trained floor directors? We were determined to teach that bird to say something if it was the last thing we or the bird did. It nearly turned out to be both.

"How about Cap'n Puget?" I suggested, watching Tim drop a sugar cube into his cup of coffee.

"How about him!" Tim answered.

"No," I replied, " I mean how about teaching Barney to say Cap'n Puget?"

There was a pause, then Tim said; "Nawww, that's too complicated. The bird could never do it. Besides," Tim added, "it should be something that will surprise McCune."

"Yes, and whatever it is should be something he'll say on the air," I added. We both laughed at the thought.

A couple of days went by before we came up with just the right thing. Then it took almost the entire year to teach the bird to say it. This might have been because of our technique, but more likely it was Barney's resistance to any socializing influence.

Teaching a parrot to talk is a lot like potty training a child...you know it's going to happen, you're just not sure when. In the case of Barney it happened in the summer, but not on the air as we had hoped. Frankly, had he said it on the air, Tim and I would have finished our broadcast careers then and there.

As it turned out, Barney squawked out his speech in the studio one afternoon just before the show was to go on the air. The studio was lighted, Cap'n Puget was sitting on the bench in the alcove and Barney was atop the diver's helmet. Tim and I were putting the finishing touches to the set. Then it happened.

"Squaaawk....KING-TV....squaaawk KING-TV!"

The studio was frozen in time, the crew unable to comprehend what they thought they had just heard. Then a murmur as everyone asked everyone what the bird just said...everyone but Tim and me, that is. We knew darn well what the parrot said and it was all we could do to keep from collapsing in laughter. I suspect McCune knew what the bird said and wasn't about to have Barney repeat himself...especially this close to going on the air.

Much to our relief, Barney kept his beak shut for the rest of the program, but for some reason Cap'n Puget wasn't quite himself throughout the show.

7

Barney died about six years later without ever repeating himself. And Cap'n Puget never mentioned the incident again, nor did he let anyone know how much time he spent trying to unteach the parrot.

CHAPTER 3

Send in the Clowns!

Oddly enough Barney wasn't the only parrot in my journalistic life. The other parrot came along fourteen years later in an episode with the staff clown. Every office has a staff clown, you know. He or she is the person who puts shaving cream on the earpiece of your telephone handset, then calls you up. Or calls the assignment desk to report a bunch of police cars at South Angela and Eddy Streets....which turns out to be the South Precinct of the Police Department. Whoever remembers the address of the Police Station? It's just there...downtown!

I have chosen not to name the staff clown. He or she might want to work somewhere else...and probably is.

The story: The parrot was a lot like Barney...It just sat around and pried open sunflower seeds. I couldn't help thinking what irony it was that the bird couldn't or wouldn't talk and his owner was a journalist. The owner was single and when he went on vacation parked the bird anywhere he could, most often with a secretary. This was one of those times.

The bird was confined to a large metal cage...too large to be tucked neatly away in a corner. So to get it out of the way and prevent the staff from spending too much time trying to teach the bird to talk, the cage was placed in Howard's office. Howard was the news department's business manager, a man who was always there to lend a hand, give a word of encouragement and take a joke. Howard didn't mind sharing his office with a parrot, as long as the bird was quiet. Just to make sure, Howard put a cover over the cage. It was just a precaution, because after all the parrot, like Barney, couldn't talk. Or could he?

Everyone knows that parrots can talk, right? And they're all named "Polly," right? Our staff clown counted on Howard believing just that. No sooner had the parrot been placed in Howard's office when Howard said "...Polly want a cracker!" Talk about predictable. Smiling, the staff clown went to his desk and removed a small black tape recorder from the drawer. He walked to an empty room down the hall from the news room, then using his best "parrot" voice recorded some choice comments. When he'd finished he rewound the tape to exactly one minute before the recorded voice.

It was almost an hour before the opportunity presented itself and the staff clown entered Howard's office...on the pretext of checking his vacation schedule or something of that sort. As he sat down, he put the tape recorder under the covered cage and turned it on. It took a mere thirty seconds to conduct his business and he was gone.

It was quiet...very quite for a news room. That's because most of the people there were in on the gag and were anxiously waiting for the tape to reach its message.

10

Howard worked diligently at his desk, unaware of the unusual silence. His head was down, his mind submerged in the paperwork arrayed on his desk. It was quiet, very quite.

Then it happened.

"Sqwaaaaak......sqwaaaaak," went the high pitch of the imitator's voice. "Sqwaaaak.......go to H——, Howard.....go to H——!"

Howard stopped working. A titter waffed through the news room. The voice continued;

"Howard, you're an idiot....sqwaaaaak.......go to H——!"

Howard slowly peered up from his work, slightly red faced, not wishing to react too suddenly as if to prove the parrot right. He looked around...no one was looking, so he reached over and slowly picked up the cover of the cage.

"Sqwaaaaaak!"

Then he saw it, the tiny black tape recorder sitting next to the cage. He'd been had all right, he knew it and everyone in the news room knew it. And everybody was laughing, everybody but the parrot that is, you see, the parrot couldn't talk.

CHAPTER 4

"What's New at the Zoo?"

My first encounter with animals in television occurred in Spokane at KXLY-TV. I include it here because it's an interesting story, serving as an illustration for would-be journalists to take nothing for granted.

What really upset our promotion director was the fact that the other two stations in town were "killing" us in the children's programming department and they were doing it with little or no effort. One station had a guy dressed up in a sailor suit. He told jokes and introduced cartoons. Across town, the children's programming wasn't even that good. But ours was worse!

With that the promotion director felt sure he could convince the station's management that now was a great time to capture once and for all the children's television market in Spokane.

He was convinced that any children's television show must have an animal in order to be successful. As proof he cited Stan Boreson in Seattle who sang, told jokes and played straight man to an aging bassett hound named NOMO. The promotion director reasoned that one dog in the state was enough. And who would tune in to a cat? So cats were out too. What the station needed, he told management, was something totally different, so curious that it would attract audiences and delight the children.

The promotion department had a budget of fifty-thousand dollars with which to develop its "capture-the-children's-market-once-and-for-all" children's program.

Just what possessed the department to decide on a wallaby isn't known, nor is anyone telling if they do. What the heck is a wallaby? It's a good question, especially if this is your first job in television and wallaby wasn't a part of your college curriculum. I'll ask again, "What the heck is a wallaby?" It is a small member of the kangaroo family. Ok, but not to sound too stupid, this next question is fundamental, "Where does one get a wallaby...besides New Zealand or Australia?"

"We're in the advertising business, are we not?" the promotion director asked. Then without waiting for an answer said, "Then we advertise!"

Of course, I thought to myself. How silly of me, we'll just put an ad in the Wild Kingdom News. Is he for real?

Two weeks later, maybe three, the station received a call from the San Diego Zoo. It seems they had a young male wallaby they would be happy to sell to our station. A deal was struck. Talk about faith, it was a sight-unseen deal, after all you can't make a lot of trips to San Diego to check out wallabies. The deal was this; the wallaby would be shipped to Spokane and a check would be shipped to San Diego. With the joy that comes only from having pulled off the deal of the century, the promotion director informed management that they were the proud parents of a

sixteen-pound wallaby and the station was on its way
to capturing, once and for all, the children's television
programming market in Spokane!

The wallaby, of course, was to be the main attraction, with the host, Jack, the straight man. And the
show was appropriately called Mr. Wallaby and Jack.

After Mister Wallaby was paid for, the rest of the
money was used to launch an advertising campaign,
one that would make "Mister Wallaby and Jack" as
common as Simon and Schuster, Smith and Wesson...
Anyway, you get the point. There were radio and TV
ads, not just on our station but on every station in
town, not to mention the billboards, magazines and
newspapers. The program went on the air as planned.
No problems and even Jack was excited. It was almost
too good to be true. And needless to say with all the
hoopla and pre-program publicity, the audience for
that first show was huge...and it stayed that way.
Mister Wallaby and Jack was a giant "hit"...KXLY-TV
had accomplished what it set out to do...capture once-
and-for-all the children's television market in
Spokane.

But alas, as those of us in the television broadcasting business eventually know, nothing lasts
forever.

When Mister Wallaby wasn't on the air or with
one of the many staffers who adored dragging him
home for an overnight, he was kept at an animal shelter on the city's east side. It was a comfortable, open
area where people could come by and see the wallaby
during the day, amidst signs promoting the TV show.

Six months after the show began, Jack and Mister
Wallaby were doing very well. Personal appearances
and testimonials translated to fame and fortune for
them, fortune in terms of good ratings and a major
share of the children's television market.

I was working the night shift in the television news room alone, just me and a couple of police monitors and a typewriter. The phone rang.

"News room," I said.

"You alone?', the voice on the other end asked.

"I'm always alone on this shift," I replied. "What's up?"

It was one of the studio engineers, a friend who occasionally called or stopped by to talk. There was a pause. Then cautiously, he suggested I grab a camera and in his words, "Come out here on the double!"

"Here" was the animal shelter where Mister Wallaby made his home. My heart sank at the thought that something dreadful might have happened to the wallaby.

"Is Mister Wallaby hurt or something?" I blurted out, "Is he dead?"

"I can't tell you over the phone," he said, "just grab a camera and get out here...fast."

I hung up, grabbed my coat and camera and headed out to the east side of town. It seemed like it took all night to get there and as I drove all sorts of things were going through my mind. What could it be? I wondered. Whatever it was, it would be news. The promotion department had done a great job. The wallaby was a winner, a local hero... and anything it did was news...or anything that was done to it was news. I repressed my worst fears.

When I arrived, Jim, the man who called me, was waiting near the cage. He was smiling. Smiling! My God he was smiling. Didn't he know that I had just gone through some of the worst moments of my life? What could be so urgent while at the same time prompting Jim to smile? I was mildly irritated so say the least.

I got the camera and some lights and walked over to the cage and Smilin' Jim.

"Okay," I said, "What's so darn important?"

"Look for yourself," he said, still smiling.

I did look...and then I began to smile. I couldn't believe my eyes. Then I began to laugh..a whole lot. Then, after pulling myself together I began to film what I saw, trying not to jiggle the camera with my chuckling. I began to laugh more when it ocurred to me that the promotion director wouldn't be laughing when we showed him this film of Mister Wallaby giving birth to a baby, right next to a sign that said "Male Wallaby."

The promotion director was down, but not out. No self-respecting promotion man would let a thing like this get the better of him. Oh, he shed a tear or two but in no time at all pulled himself together and vowed to quickly save the sinking ship. He immediately got some more dollars and launched another advertising campaign. Of course he waited until the collective laughter died down. When it had, the billboards declared a brand new capture-the-children's-television-market-once-and-for-all program entitled...."The Wallabies and Jack." Genius, absolute genius!

It was rumored that the folks at the San Diego Zoo were grinning all the way to the bank, mumbling something about P.T. Barnum being alive and well in the Pacific Northwest.

CHAPTER 5

Ivan, the Terrible!

Like children's programs, commercials cost a lot of money to produce. The announcer must be paid, and props cost money, as do the cameramen and studio personnel and it takes a buck or two to use the studio. The costs are usually "block" costs, based on an hourly rate or group of hours. So it pays for the producer to be as productive as possible. The old adage "time is money" is never more true than in the production of television commercials.

One of the more frequent users of television studio time for commercial production was the B & I Circus Store, a large department store complex in Tacoma. Hardly a day passed that a B & I spot didn't appear on the air...somewhere...sometime. All of the B & I commercials were produced in KOMO Television studios. And like many businesses using television, the B & I had its own announcer who was recognized as the B & I Spokesperson. He was a jovial sort, a bit plumpish who was liked by everybody and when not doing the B & I spots, was either running for office or managing the B & I Stereo Department.

He called everybody "podner"...it was "podner" this, "podner" that and while it was just his way, it drove me crazy. But not nearly as crazy as another of his commercial quirks...animals. He must have been really impressed by Ralph Williams and his dog Storm, because Mister B & I was intent on using an animal in his commercials. A big animal.

"Meet Ivan," he said to me one day, "Go ahead, shake his hand."

Nobody moved. There were no takers, just gawkers as the studio crew stood around looking at his three hundred pound gorilla companion, Ivan. The animal had a heavy chain around his neck with the other end attached to the hand of his handler. It was never quite clear, however, just who handled who.

I don't recall exactly what the B&I commercial was going to say...something about going "ape" over the prices and deals, I suspect. But a gorilla? What in the heck were we going to do with a three hundred pound gorilla? Wrong question. What was a three hundred pound gorilla going to do with us?

The plan involved putting Ivan on the set with Mister B&I, with the camera picking up shots of both at the appropriate times. You know, when the announcer says, "You'll go ape, podner," the camera switches to Ivan who is sitting nearby ripping a floor director limb from limb. Just out of camera range was Ivan's handler still holding the chain.

It was during one of the "takes" in making the commercial that Ivan spied the battens, the network of pipes above the studio from which the lights were suspended. It was sort of like a steel and wood jungle.

Suddenly, without warning...not unlike those final scenes from King Kong where he climbs the Empire State Building, Ivan jerked the chain from the handler and was away...up the walls and onto the battens, disappearing into the maze of lights, wires and cross members. Ivan was no longer in our territory, intimidated by the cameras, handlers and the announcer calling everyone "podner." No sireee, Ivan was in HIS element and while not a jungle of the green and wet variety, it was territory few of us could handle.

There we were in sort of an African stand-off, the studio crew on the floor looking up trying to figure out what to do...and Ivan above us swinging from light to light.

"Get a banana!" someone suggested.

Wonderful, I thought, *and just who's going to hand the banana to him?*

Well...looking back on all this, Ivan reminded me a lot of my dog. He wasn't going to return until he was good and ready, bananas or no bananas. Ivan did eventually come down, perhaps because he didn't like what he saw from up there.

We were all relieved, all except the announcer who left the studio mumbling something about getting this stupid monkey off his back....podner![3]

---

[3] When not doing commercials Ivan was caged at the B & I Circus Store and because of that became the object of animal rights activists wanting him freed or placed in a proper zoo. At one time, entertainer Michael Jackson was reported to have offered Ivan a home on his California ranch.

CHAPTER 6

A Whale of a Tale to Tell!

While it is true animals often provide the best materials for stories, not all such stories are funny, nor do they all have happy endings. But they are all unique. None more so than the story of Namu the Killer Whale, or more to the point, KOMO-TV's coverage of Namu the Killer Whale.

In the summer of 1965 the big news of the day was the capture of a two-ton killer whale by some fishermen off the coast of British Columbia at a place called Namu. Upon hearing the news the curator of Seattle's Aquarium announced he was going to Namu and attempt to bring the whale back to Seattle....alive. It would be a race since the fishermen were more inclined to kill the beast than save it for science, since killer whales were known to wipe out salmon runs. For whatever reason, maybe the heat, but more likely the need for diversion, the entire populace of the Puget Sound Region caught the spirit of the chase and the annual summer celebration known as Seafair ended up playing second banana to a whale.

It was no surprise then that while the aquarium was getting ready to retrieve its prize, the region's radio and television stations began covering the story as if it were an event of worldwide significance. Doctor Tag Gornell, a veterinarian, became a local hero by virtue of appearing daily on radio and television as a "Namu" expert. Bob Hardwick, then among the best known Seattle disc jockeys, offered his own boat to tow the whale back to Seattle. The offer was accepted.[4]

Technically bringing the whale back to Seattle wasn't a big deal. The whale was to be herded into a large floating cage which was closed with wire mesh on the sides and bottom. It was held afloat by sealed fifty gallon drums. The cage, with the whale inside, was towed back to Seattle, but the whale inside actually swam back!

I had been back at the studio less than an hour after working a remote broadcast at the Seattle Center, when I was called upstairs to the program director's office.

"How would you like to be the talent on the whale remote?" he asked.

"The what?"I replied.

"The whale remote," he repeated. I knew very well what he was talking about. Those of us down in the studio had been thinking about doing something like that ourselves. But I was surprised to hear that "upstairs" was way ahead of everybody and had long ago discussed the possibility of doing such a remote broadcast.

---

4 Hardwick's boat was too small to pull the cage and a large Foss tugboat was contracted to do the job. Hardwick remained with the flotilla, however, doing his morning broadcasts from his boat.

The station, I learned, had already leased a tug-boat from the Foss Company and intended to place on it a self-contained operational television station that would link up to land by way of a microwave signal. What I was hearing was space-age stuff and as far as anyone knew at the time, nothing like this had ever been done before.

The plans called for us to board the tug on Sunday morning, proceed north through Elliott Bay and Puget Sound and rendezvous with Namu's flotilla on the other side of Deception Pass north of Whidbey Island. It was Friday, lots of time to gather some gear and notify my family, so the rest of the day was spent loading the tug with equipment. Field producer of the expedition was Tom Rogstad (the station's Program Director), and for the next six hours he, along with the remote's chief engineer Fred Fowler, directed me, Roy Sillence, Warren Wilson and Bill Seidel, as we made trip after trip between the station and Pier 70 carrying what must have been tons of television equipment.

On Saturday, my usual day off, I stopped by the station to find that the schedule had been moved up and we were to leave for Deception Pass as soon as we could get aboard the tugboat.

"Where in the heck have you been?" Rogstad asked, "We've been trying to get you for a couple of hours!"

I explained that I had been at the library reading up on whales and that if I were to go now someone had better notify my wife and get some clothes to the station.

"Already done!" Rogstad stated.

Our studio and home for the next five days was the tugboat *Lorna Foss* and it took some doing to make it a studio. At the top of the wheelhouse, some fifty feet above the water was a large microwave "dish" with which we would send sound and pictures

25

to shore. Just below and slightly behind....atop the cabin actually...was a full-size black and white studio camera. There was barely enough room for the camera, not to mention the operator. A mere yard or two away from the camera was a makeshift audio bench on which was the microphone equipment. It takes a lot more to make a picture than a dish, an audio bench and a camera. A bunch of "other," highly sensitive electronic equipment had to be stored aboard the tug which was already crowded with its normal crew of five, five newspeople and a makeshift studio.

"This stuff has to be protected from the weather!" It was our chief engineer.

"What do you suggest?" Rogstad replied, some mild frustration in his voice. After all both he and Fowler had checked out just about every available space.

"Wellll," Fowler dragged the word out as he thought the problem through. "The captain's cabin would be perfect." He was kidding...wasn't he? Maybe it's okay to go down with the ship, but giving up one's cabin.....

Most of the sensitive electronic stuff was placed on the Captain's bunk so it would ride out any rough weather without damage. The rest of the equipment was put on his dresser and the floor. So where did the captain sleep? Not anywhere he wanted this time: he bunked on the deck with the rest of us.

We left Seattle's Pier 71 late Saturday afternoon. It was about five, I think, a beautiful day with few clouds, one of those days that makes living on or near the Puget Sound worth every drop of rain. We arrived at Burrows Bay, just on the other side of Deception Pass, at one-fifteen Sunday morning. During the trip north, we broadcast three stories back to Seattle, two of which were short, less than a minute long to let folks know what we were doing. The third was a more elaborate report for the late news. It was incredible, really. By beaming a signal to a receiving dish on the KOMO tower atop Queen Anne Hill, viewers were able to to see a "live" picture from the fantail of a tugboat as it steamed through Puget Sound. In less than ten hours from start to finish, we had installed a complete television station aboard a tugboat, checked it out and begun broadcasting. Today such remotes are commonplace thanks to satellites, but in 1964, such a feat was revolutionary.

For obvious reasons our spirits were high as we left the Seattle waterfront. Rogstad jokingly remarked..."Well, if it doesn't work, we can just keep on going!" We laughed. It was easy to laugh, because it was working.

We didn't sleep much that first night. We were wide awake for the journey north and once there spent most of the time watching the whale inside the pen.

In the morning two of our crew had to go ashore. Our radio wasn't working and we had to notify the microwave shore station to move to another position. You see, microwave, in order to broadcast, must be line-of-sight which means the shore crew of Duncan McKenna and Ed Werdon had to follow the flotilla on land, moving frequently to positions where they could be seen and we could see them. A telescope mounted on the tug's microwave dish was used to sight a similar dish atop a small van driven by Werdon and McKenna. During the entire remote broadcast, which lasted a week and consisted of hundreds of broadcasts, there was a less than two percent picture loss. The credit goes in no small part to our dish operator Warren Wilson who was never more than a few feet from the dish in his ever-present orange life vest. It seems Warren neglected to tell anyone that he didn't know how to swim.

We broadcast a live report from the tugboat every hour. These reports were about a minute in length. Then each evening we recapped the day's events with a half hour program which at times was aired from the studio...other times from the tug as it followed the flotilla.

By the time we departed Burrows Bay for home, the flotilla had grown considerably. The small private craft offered by Bob Hardwick was not quite up to the job, so at this time it was replaced with another tug from the Foss Company. There was our TV tug, of course, which at times was as much an attraction as the whale. And there were hundreds of smaller boats, bearing the curious mostly, that showed up each day. There were other media too—newspapers, magazines, radio and TV stations—most of whom showed up in float planes which were making almost hourly passes over us.

Because we didn't have a whale in tow, we were free to move around and most of the time we steamed alongside the other tug and Namu. Occasionally Skipper Skip Lampman would guide the *Lorna Foss* close to the pen and we were able to get very good pictures of the whale. Bill Seidel fashioned several small underwater microphones called hydrophones, which when lowered into the water near the pen, allowed us to pick up and broadcast back to the station the actual sounds of Namu.

On the subject of sound....well, there were times when not everything worked as it should have worked. I was on the fantail one evening, my usual spot for the evening broadcast "home." It was to be a "live" shot and we established beforehand that I would take my cues from a television monitor placed just out of camera range but where I could easily see it. Murphy's Law applies in the broadcast business, too, and the TV monitor went out. I couldn't hear or see anything from the news anchors and would be unable to respond when they cued to me on the boat. But not to worry, Seidel could hear the program and could simply replay the cue to me. There would, of course, be a slight delay but nothing that would bother the audience. Now just how to relay the cue was the mystery. Seidel could yell at me. But since we were setting the industry standard for remote broadcasting, yelling was not appropriate.

It was Rogstad, I think, who came up with the idea of cueing me by blowing the tug's whistle. It worked! But it sure sounded funny, like one of those children's records that says, "...turn the page when you hear the whistle!"

"Now, from aboard the *Lorna Foss*, here with his live report is Bill Brubaker....BEEEEEEP! Good evening....."

For five days and four nights our intrepid little television crew braved the seas...which isn't saying much since the weather was great and the water was like a mill pond. And, except for finding a place to sleep only now and then, we had all the comforts of home. One of those comforts was food. A typical lunch, as I recall, was choice beef or pork roast with all the trimmings and apple pie for dessert. Skipper Skip said that when it comes to food on a tugboat...every day is Sunday. He wasn't kidding.

At one point in our journey the onboard generator that supplied all the power to the television equipment quit! Now you have to know that when TV techs as good as those in our crew couldn't fix it...it couldn't be fixed. The only decent thing left to do was...burial at sea.

It was quite a ceremony really. Engineering Chief Fowler said a few appropriate words...none of which are printable....then with sleight of foot launched the errant generator into the deep six.

"It fell overboard? What do ya mean it fell overboard?" It was Fred's boss on the other end of the radio.

"Over!"

"I don't know what happened, " Fred said, "one minute it was there and the next minute it was gone!"

Fred was no dummy. He knew that the only way to get a new generator was not to have one in his possession at the time he asked for a new one. Follow me? Apparently Fred's boss didn't, because a new generator was immediatley dispatched from the station to a rendezvous point on the north end of Camano Island. The truck arrived at a deserted beach in the dead of night. Skipper Skip beached the tug and what unfolded next was a scene right out of a Howard Hawkes war movie. On the beach, the truck sat with its back doors open, casting light on the beach with the overhead dome from inside the truck. Several people, bathed in moonlight, waded ashore with a small dinghy in tow. They retrieved the generator, and a half dozen cases of beer...something for the ship's doctor, I think.

After five days it was over. But I'll never forget as long as I live the triumphant entry into Puget Sound. It was a bright Pacific Northwest day and every pier along Seattle's waterfront, every open space, boat, wharf and car top was jammed with people. They were standing, sitting, clinging and even hanging around just to get a glimpse of Namu, The Killer Whale, and the flotilla that followed. We spread a large KOMO-TV banner across the front of the tug. We were proud.

But our moment of glory was short lived. Soon came the reality that it was over and the equipment must go back to its places and we must go back to our jobs. We put off the task of "tearing down" for as long as possible. A written message from KOMO President W.W. Warren read:

KOMO-TV's audience experienced for the first time, a top, continuing news story, over a period of several days, live and direct. Opportunities for this kind of local service of such community-wide interest are rare and we can all take pride that KOMO-TV recognized the potential in the story and met the challenge to go out and get it!

Yes it was a great service...and yes it was a technical milestone. And true, it demonstrated the company's resolve to be a leader. But most of all, Mister Warren, it was great fun!

CHAPTER 7

Milk and Cookies!

In twenty-five years of hanging around television news rooms, I observed one unchanging thing: news people eat anything that isn't nailed down, on paper or under a desk protector. I mean anything and it doesn't even have to be edible. I recall a producer of the late news who brought a hundred sugar cookies into the news room and placed them on the production desk. One hundred sugar cookies! Ten minutes later the large plastic bowl containing the cookies was as empty as an assignment editor's heart. Think of it... ten cookies a minute.

It's during the holidays, however, that news people really demonstrate their ability to scarf...whole turkeys picked to the bone in minutes, fruit cakes reduced to nothing more than a wisp of crumbs atop the news desk, and candy...candy doesn't stand a chance— seconds I would say...yes, seconds and it is gone.

I once covered a story at the National Marine Fisheries Building on Seattle's Portage Bay where the government was experimenting in high protein foods for third world countries. The high protein in this case came from fish, which was ground to a fine meal, and then added to prepared foods. For our story the fish meal was added to cookies. They weren't bad actually...and you couldn't taste the fish meal, unless you thought about it a lot.

Being a dutiful reporter, I packed up a dozen or so cookies and brought them back to the news room. There was, you see, an unwritten and unspoken code among journalists that when anything is offered free, you accept it and in doing so you accept for everyone in the news room. After all, when someone else gets goodies you should be able to share in them as well. It's called the Unwritten, Unspoken Code of the Free-bie!

When I took the cookies back to the news room to the newsies whose salivary glands were in overdrive, I carefully explained that the cookies were made with fish meal. Without even blinking, my co-workers went right to it and in seconds the platter was clean. Now you would think that the Unwritten, Unspoken Code of the Freebie wouldn't apply to one's own lunch, Wrong!

Across the street from the TV station was a small Vietnamese eatery called Cafe Loc which dished up the most wonderful and exotic dishes that you could stuff into a paper carton. The delicious smell in the news room was a dead giveaway that lunch was being served. No sooner had the aroma reached the news room when seldom-used desk drawers produced forks, spoons, and even chopsticks. It was crazy, you didn't even have to be hungry; if its free...eat it!

One female staffer was particularly adept at applying the Code. Anytime and every time Ruth Walsh received or retrieved edibles while on assignment, she would bring them back to the news room to be shared by all. She was wonderful. Never, never

34

would you find Ruth out in the news car, after covering the watermelon festival, trying to eat the evidence. Some have, believe me, some have.

Ruth was also good at sharing someone else's good hunting. I think she had a fork AND a spoon in her desk. Anyway, there was a time when her willingness to share and her willingness to partake got the best of her. Yet another story about cookies.

Reporter Ed Evans had gone to the University of Washington to check out a story about using earthworms as a protein substitute. The experimenter believed that adding chopped earthworms to other foods would be of great benefit to the world. Like his predecessors at the National Marine Fisheries Agency, the "professor" added the substance to cookies. The major and disgusting difference, Ed found, was that the worms were not ground into meal, but chopped into small pieces that when mixed with the cookie dough looked like chocolate chips. You're getting ahead of me!

Ed did the story and true to the Unwritten, Unspoken Code of the Freebie packed several dozen chocolate-chip-look-alike cookies back to the news room where he placed them on the counter. Neither Ed nor the assignment editor felt a compelling urge to tell the staff what was in the cookies. And no one thought to ask about the cookies or, for that matter, Ed's story.

It didn't take long before the ravenous staff descended on the cookie jar. The cookies were gone in a matter of seconds and among those nibbling away was Ruth. Time passed.

In addition to being a fine reporter, Ruth was an anchor person and it was during the anchor phase of her daily schedule that she learned the awful truth. As is routine Ed wrote the story and turned it over to the producer who, among other tasks, assigned the stories to be read. Ruth got the worm cookie story.

"There's something new in what's good for you," she read, "Now here with the story is reporter Ed Evans."

As Ed unfolded his story in words and pictures, she slowly began to realize that the cookies she had eaten earlier that afternoon were not chocolate chip cookies. Funny, they looked like chocolate chip cookies, and the reporter said they looked like chocolate chip cookies, but in fact they were worm cookies. She had been had!

It makes one wonder how many of the quarter million viewers adjusted their color frantically when they saw an anchor woman with pale green skin.

CHAPTER 8

Ladies in Waiting

The power of television to influence society is never more apparent than in times of social upheaval. During the Cuban and subsequent revolutions around the world, rebels typically sought to take over broadcast facilities. Even in the American revolution of the sixties, TV and radio stations were the prime targets of groups who were able to control the media by simply orchestrating marches and demonstrations to gain attention. Invariably when TV cameras went away, so did the demonstration. On rare occasions in this country groups have attempted to make their point by actually taking over a broadcast.

Enter "Lesbians For Peace," who would have been successful had they known anything about television.

About the time the evening news was scheduled to go on the air, a young woman entered the station, milled about the lobby for a moment or two and asked the receptionist if she could use the ladies room. She was directed to the rear of the building, but did not go to the ladies room, selecting instead the adjacent alley door where parked outside was a large bus filled with her friends. She opened the door and let them in, protest signs and all.

In the studio less than thirty feet away, our news program had been on the air about eight minutes and we were into the first commercial break. There were two studios, in fact, the entrances for which were side by side. Above each of the doors lighted signs would tell a would-be interloper if the program was "On-The-Air" or in a "Standby" mode. Now the one over Studio B, the studio in which the news was being aired was lighted...it read "ON-THE-AIR." Now it doesn't take a rocket scientist to figure out that when the "On-The-Air" light is on, the program is probably...on the air, and when it's off, it isn't.

The Lesbians For Peace could have used a rocket scientist, because they waited until the "On-The-Air" light went off before bursting into the studio, sans signs and slogans. How considerate, I mused later, they didn't want to interrupt the program!

I had just cued to a ninety-second commercial break by saying..."We'll be right back after this." As I looked up from my copy I saw the studio doors fly open behind the camera and the Lesbians For Peace began to file into the room. I still don't know why, but I sensed something was about to go terribly wrong, so when the women entered I sprang from my chair and walked quickly past them, out the same door and into the control room across the hall.

The Lesbians For Peace circled in front of the podium behind which I once stood, and they faced the camera. Since we were still in the commercial break, the audience had no idea anything was amiss. They made no effort to stop me, probably because they didn't even know who I was or what I did for a living.

About thirty seconds of the break had passed. A minute to go.

I made my way back through the protestors, out the same door through which they entered and into an announcers booth, a small studio equipped with tape machines, turntables and a microphone from which the announcer could make station breaks every half hour. I explained to the announcer on duty that the studio had just been taken over by Lesbians For Peace and that I intended to finish the news from here. We put a slide on the screen that read KOMO-TV News Special. I told the director to roll the newsfilm on cue just as if I were on camera in the studio, and that I would make some sort of disclaimer that due to technical difficulties the live studio portion of the broadcast had been interrupted. I could hardly announce the real reason.

When the commercial break ended we went to slide and I rattled off the disclaimer, followed by the news. It worked like a charm.

Meanwhile, back in the studio, our uninvited guests were preparing to make a statement in front of what they thought were "live" cameras. They were not. The director of the program however had rolled a tape to record the statement, while the news went merrily on the air.

The Lesbians For Peace would never have known the truth had the News Director not told them. But being a fair minded sort, he agreed to air a portion of the statement in the next news program which would be at eleven that evening.

It worked out pretty well...the protestors were able to make a statement and we finished the news. As for KOMO, management's concern was manifested in a memo declaring the rest rooms off-limits to anyone except employees.

CHAPTER 9

Bombs Awaaaay!

There are other ways to get attention. Bomb threats are one way and they used to work. But over time station managers came to ignore them, primarily because if you reported them as news items, other crazies would find making them great sport. Nevertheless television and radio stations have been common targets for such threats and, on rare occasions, actual bombs.

Our staff was even less prone to react to bomb threats, especially if they occurred in the middle of something...like dinner. On Thanksgiving Day, 1966, KOMO's Home Economist Katherine Wise had prepared, just for the night crew, a beautiful Thanksgiving feast, complete with roast turkey, oyster dressing, mashed potatoes, gravy, creamed onions and pumpkin pie. It was a tradition whereby each Christmas and Thanksgiving Katherine prepared two complete holiday dinners. The first was prepared as part of her daily television program and given to the day crew. The second was prepared just for the night crew.

The schedule that day, like most holidays, was light. We came to work about four, did a couple of shows, Katherine's and Captain Puget's as I recall, then we were off until the late show at eleven. We had set up a large table in the middle of the studio complete with white linen and were seated around it enjoying our drumsticks and giblet gravy when the receptionist burst through the studio doors to inform us she had just received a bomb threat from a caller who said the bomb would go off in an hour. The initial reaction was what you might expect of a top notch television studio crew...nothing.

"Pass the cranberry sauce, please."

There was general agreement, while not spoken, that if anyone really wanted to bomb the place, they would hardly warn us, and besides we had an hour.

The crew chief told all those in the station who wished to leave, they could do so. Some did. Meanwhile, a quick search was made of the building, and the others stayed behind and polished off the oyster dressing and jello salad.

It was, of course, proper to notify the "higher-ups" and they in turn would notify the authorities.

We finished the pumpkin pie just as the police and station's Chief Executive, W.W. Warren, arrived. They searched but found no bomb. What they did find was the crew seated around a large table in the middle of the studio enjoying coffee. In the middle of the table was the remains of a once large and meaty bird.

W.W. stood there for a moment and then said: "Don't you people know there's been a bomb threat?"

"Yes sir!", came the reply.

"You're not worried about it?"

The crew looked at one another, then back to W.W.

"Nope." The answer came in unison.

W.W. looked perplexed."Was the turkey good?" he asked.

Everyone nodded.

W.W. turned and headed for the door, his last words something about fringe benefits, and he was gone.

Bomb threats, it would seem, were taken a bit more seriously at our sister station in Portland, Oregon. There the standard procedure was to forcefully evacuate the building immediately.

Word reached us that one Monday morning in 1973 staff members in Portland quietly but firmly went from department to department telling employees to vacate the building. There was no panic and the employees filed out of the building and waited across the street for the all-clear.

There had been hardly enough time to conduct a thorough search before the employees were told to go back to work. What was up?

It was simple...the station manager had received in his Monday morning mail a memo from the receptionist that there had been a bomb threat. She stated further in her note that the man who called said the bomb would go off before noon. That was all the station manager needed to spring into action. Evacuate the building was the order.

The threat had actually been phoned in on Saturday morning, threatening detonation at noon that day. But, through delays, the message didn't reach management until two days later.

I wonder what must have gone through the caller's mind?

Ted Garlatz Sr

Larry Nelson

CHAPTER 10

Two Wrongs Don't Make a Right....Unless You're The One That's Right! Right?

The Federal Communications Commission, the big brother of the broadcast business, has always been clear about broadcasting false information. The regulations state that under no circumstances will you, as a broadcaster, intentionally broadcast information that is wrong or misleading. If you do the penalties range from a verbal warning to having one's broadcast license revoked.

And just as there are prohibitions against broadcasting false information, there are rules against using broadcast information for private gain.

Two wrongs!

KOMO Radio, like many stations in markets the size of Seattle, has an airborne traffic spotter...a keen-of-eye, blond-of-hair, lantern-jawed aviator who each morning before dawn defies the laws of gravity and death. And that's just getting to the airport! Once in the air this broadcasting birdman reports on the hourly migration of workers in and out of the city. The station's first traffic pilot was John Caughlin who darted here and there above town in a low-wing

Mooney, a plane that was too fast and had the added disadvantage of a lower wing that often obscured traffic below.

After John came Ted Garlatz, who in later years would share the controls with his son Ted Junior. While KOMO's master of morning mirth Larry Nelson called both of them "Garflaps," he distinguished between the two by referring to the younger as "Teddy."

The flying career of Ted Senior would itself provide ample material for a book or two. Let's face it, any aviator who stopped counting his flying hours years before, doesn't reach that stage without surviving some of the more "horrorflying" aspects of aviation. There was, for example, the time he took off from Boeing Field with the tow bar still attached to the nose wheel of his airplane. No big deal, he said, just a lot of noise. Frankly at 4:30 in the morning he was lucky to find the airplane. Another time he was approaching the runway when he wandered into the wing-tip vortices of a Boeing 747 that had just landed. (These are whirlwinds that roll off the wings of large airplanes and the larger the plane the more severe the whirlwind.) Ted's airplane weighed about twenty-three hundred pounds and suddenly, with the runway laid out in front of him, he found himself upside down.

One of the more memorable moments came in the late sixties, one spring morning as Ted Senior was airborne doing his traffic thing. The procedure was that Ted and the announcer back at the station coordinated traffic reports over VHF Radio before going on the air. The announcer, Jay Ward this particular morning, was supposed to "cue" Ted and flip a switch.

"Now here's Ted with the latest traffic in and around the University of Washington campus."

"Roger, Jay," came the reply, "I'm over the University....er hold it, Jay, ...I'm going down!"

Silence. A stunned Jay Ward just sat there not knowing what to say. He was no aviator, but the words "...going down" were clear enough.

Finally after what must have seemed an eternity to Jay, he called for Ted. There was no answer. He put on a record and kept trying to reach his traffic spotter over VHF. There was nothing, not even static. Whatever the reason, the airplane's radio was dead. Jay began to seriously worry about the welfare of Ted Garlatz Senior.

Another eternity and the phone rang. No doubt a fan or the station's manager calling to find out what happened, Jay thought.

"It's me, Ted!" the voice on the other end answered.

"Are you ok? what happened? where are you?" Jay shot over the phone.

"I set the plane down in the Montlake parking lot," Ted explained, "The engine quit!"

It turned out ok, Ted was uninjured and believe it or not the FAA allowed him to fly the plane out of the lot and back to Boeing Field.

Ten years and a whole lot of traffic reports later, Ted was still in the air and on the air. Larry Nelson had replaced Jay Ward in the booth, and traffic reports aside, Ted and Larry over the years made morning radio in Seattle fun. But it was not what they said on the air, but what they did off the air one day that brought Ted and Larry one of their finest hours.

Larry had long suspected that other stations in the market had been monitoring off-the-air conversations between Ted and him, the remarks made in "setting up" traffic reports. He also believed the stations were using that information for their own on-the-air traffic and news reports. The other guys were not going to admit they were pirating information and who would expect them to stop doing something they wouldn't admit doing. Larry and Ted saw no alternative except to outsmart them!

It was a Thursday morning, I recall. Ted and Larry were in their usual good humor, bantering back and forth between records, setting up the next traffic report. It was during one of those "set-ups" that Larry said.

"Hey Ted....we've got a report of a tanker truck overturned on the Evergreen Point Floating Bridge!"

"Okeee-Dokey," Ted replied, "I'm on my way."

The morning listeners heard none of this of course, since it was a conversation between the two of them over VHF. As the program progressed, Ted and Larry continued their "private" conversation knowing or at least suspecting that one other station was listening. Ted told Larry that he had better get ready for a traffic report since the big tanker was sprawled all over the bridge and there was oil everywhere. Ted went into great detail about the accident, none of which went out over the air.

It did, however confirm the suspicions about the "other guys." Both KING and KOL Radio wasted little time in hitting the air with a report of a gigantic truck accident on the Evergreen Point Floating Bridge. And their advice to the motoring public was, of course, to avoid the mess and use the Lacy V. Murrow Bridge. KING-TV heard the report from KING Radio and immediately dispatched a television news crew to the scene. What they found was, nothing! Nothing but the usual mish-mash of morning traffic. They called back to the station to find out where KING Radio got its information. There was no reply. Not surprising since KING Radio wasn't about to admit they got their information from KOMO Radio, the staff of which was by now enjoying a good chuckle.

That afternoon both KING-TV and Radio and KOL Radio received certificates, delivered by messenger, which read "ROYAL KOMO GOTCHA AWARDS."

"You shouldn't otta do that sort of thing," The FCC said subsequently, in a communique to us. "It's not nice."

"Yeah, we know, but....."

Funny, the Feds just don't seem to have the sense of humor those of us in the broadcasting industry have...at least when it comes to their rules.

KING-TV had a sense of humor though. That night on the Channel 5 evening news reporter 'fessed up by recounting the story and admitting KING lacked good judgment in the matter. He ended the story by stating: "...To paraphrase Abraham Lincoln...'I'm too old to cry, but it hurts too much to laugh'."

Was the whole thing worth it? I guess that depends on who you are. Ted and Larry felt it was!

Ted "Teddy" Garlatz Jr

N-91505 on the Vashon Island beach following the collision with Chopper Seven. Garlatz was un-injured. The plane never flew again.

CHAPTER 11

Bogy at Twelve O'Clock....
Make That 5 P.M.

While we're on the subject of airplanes, we should not forget one of the greatest aerial battles of the modern world that more appropiately should be entitled..."Traffic Wars!"

It was bound to happen, you see. In fact if you were a betting person, the odds were in your favor if you wagered that Seattle's various aerial traffic reporters would meet, literally, in the bluest skies you've ever seen. There were days when it appeared there was more congestion aloft than on the streets and freeways below and each morning at sunrise and each evening at quitting time this aerial drama was played out above the city.

The little red and white Cessna 150 was piloted by KVI Radio's Cliff Murphy, a soft spoken antique dealer from Black Diamond who hardly appeared to have what author Tom Wolfe called the "right stuff." As he flew KVI's morning traffic report, Cliff would occasionally waggle a wing at KOMO's Air Patrol as they passed each other in the cut behind Mercer Island.

The KOMO Air Patrol was a Blue and White Cessna 172 known to Boeing Tower as N-91505 or 505 for short. It was a good airplane considering she was on her second engine. Her controls were a bit stiff, but in the hands of Ted Garlatz Senior she was a docile lady forgiving of every inattention and forever boring holes in the Seattle air. This little blue and white plane with KOMO painted on the tail was as familiar a sight to Seattle commuters as the Space Needle.

As the years passed and Ted senior had escaped major damage to himself and his airplane, the duties of informing the public of the perils of driving to and from work fell to his son, Ted Junior...who shall, until he is 92, be forever known as "Teddy." Now there was a day when none of us were sure if Teddy would ever see 92. It's not that he wasn't a great pilot. He was. He wouldn't have been flying professionally if he were not...I wouldn't have taken instruction from him if he were not and Mister KOMO would not have hired him...if he were not. Most pilots who hold an airman's certificate are safety conscious, and what separates the men from the boys in the flying business is their ability to handle the unexpected.

It was a Friday afternoon and there he was at a thousand feet over the southern tip of Vashon Island, orbiting as they say, checking out the car ferry traffic that was building for the weekend get-away. Teddy was not alone. Also "orbiting" at a thousand feet was the KIRO-TV News Helicopter. It too was checking out the ferry traffic. It is axiomatic that two aircraft cannot occupy the same exact airspace at the same time. They tried and the result was a mid-air collision. Teddy informed the station that he had been hit by something and that he was going to land. At that time he did not know that his right wing had been chewed off by the "KIRO Copter." Shaken, but in control, Teddy made a masterful landing on a Vashon Island beach. He was uninjured.

KIRO's helicopter sustained damage in the collision as well. With the exact extent of that damage not immediatly known, pilot Bob LaPrarie took no chances and set the aircraft down on a nearby golf course. LaPrarie, reporter Bob Brannom and Photographer Lorenzo Townsend were shaken but safe.

N-91505 was totaled and could not be flown home. It was dismantled and taken off the beach in pieces.

As for the KIRO Copter...there was little doubt about it being damaged and LaPrarie wasn't sure if he could fly it back to Boeing Field or not. He would have no doubt decided not to, but the decision was made for him when a lady golfer, less than a hundred yards away, smacked a golf ball with the best five iron shot she'd ever made. She kept her head down just like the pro said she should and never saw the brightly painted flying machine directly in front of her.

"Whack!" The ball slammed into the helicopter, cracking the windscreen. A very startled pilot suddenly realized midair damage or not he wasn't going anywhere. It was later determined that while the collision did about two thousand dollars to the helicopter, the golf ball did about five thousand dollars worth and the helicopter had to be trucked off the island.

At the time the incident didn't seem very funny, especially when you think of how it might have turned out. But the fact that nobody got hurt or killed allowed a certain amount of "gallows humor" to creep into what might have been a tragedy. The newspapers had a field day and the two stations were the talk of the town. About three days after the incident, KOMO Radio received the following press release, penned no doubt, by some wit in another news room:

FOR IMMEDIATE RELEASE

The Federal Aviation Administration has released preliminary findings into the midair collision of two aircraft over Vashon Island.

At about 5:20 pm the two aircraft engaged over the target area known as "Ferry Dock." The KOMO Air Patrol, piloted by Major Ted Garlatz Junior, gained the killer position and was able to deploy one air-launched heat-seeking scone which detonated upon impact with Chopper Seven's tail rotor. As Corporal Bob Brannom was about to say; "Quite a traffic tie-up, John," Colonel Bob LaPrarie turned Chopper Seven so that waist gunner Sgt. Lorenzo Townsend could fire three hundred rounds of "Lloyd Cooney for Senator" bumper stickers at the KOMO Air Patrol.

The Air Patrol received extensive damage to the right wing and was forced down. Chopper Seven, damaged in the conflict, also set down safely.

Commander John Lippman said: "The Lloyd Cooney bumper stickers are obsolete. We are now armed with the latest 'happiness is a family home evening' bumper stickers and the next time we will not miss." Air Patrol Commander, Colonel Bryan Johnson said when asked to comment, "We have checked with our weapons designer Katherine Wise and she said all we need is a pinch more salt!"[5]

-30-
_____

[5] The Cast:
 Bob Brannom—KIRO TV News reporter
 Bob LaPrarie—Chopper 7 pilot
 Lorenzo Townsend—KIRO TV photographer
 Lloyd Cooney—former KIRO TV general manager
 John Lippman—KIRO TV news director
 Bryan Johnson—KOMO Radio news director
 Katherine Wise—KOMO home economist

CHAPTER 12

The Case of the Golden Side-cutters

In addition to being two of television's best broadcast engineers, Roy Sillence and Jim Menahan had a sense of humor which was no better displayed than at the retirement party of out-going Program Director Tom Rogstad. There were speeches, a few tears and lots of gifts, among them a pair of gold plated side-cutters mounted on a walnut base. An engraved inscription read: *To Tom Rogstad with affection, the KOMO Engineers.* Side-cutters are, for you non-engineer types, nothing more than wire cutters.

There were chuckles and a few glances askance, but nothing was said about the event or events that prompted such a touching gift. It was definitely an inside joke known only to Rogstad, the engineering staff and Mrs Bullitt's television station down the street, Channel 5 (KING-TV).

The event was the State Republican Convention that was being held in the Opera House at Seattle Center across the street from the KOMO studios. In the final moments of the convention, all three Television Stations, KOMO, KING and KIRO, were winding down their "live" coverage. KOMO-TV had finished first, the anchors had gone home and the engineering staff was "breaking down," which means they were packing up the equipment to return it to the studio.

Channel 5, meanwhile, was still in the process of "wrapping up," sending a live summary of the day's events to its audience in the Seattle area as well as to its stations in Portland and Spokane.

During any event at which more than one television station is taking part, it's smart to work together in the placement of wires, cables and electronic equipment so that they're not spread all over the place. In this case all the cables were routed from the Seattle Opera House, through a six inch standpipe, up the wall, through a roof transom and outside to the stations' three remote trucks in the parking lot. A good arrangement, it not only allowed the Opera House door to remain closed, but prevented people from walking on or tripping over cables and wires.

Since time is money in the broadcast biz, it's far more convenient to cut wires and some cables when "breaking down" than to spend a great deal of time tracing them through the standpipe and transom. The wires and cables can then be quickly pulled through, and it doesn't disturb other stations that might still be on the air...well sometimes it doesn't.

Roy and Jim were up to their armpits in six inch conduit, side-cutters in hand, cutting and snipping up a storm. Among the miles of wires and cables strung by KOMO were miles of wires and cables strung by the other guys, including a twelve-pair wire—twelve individual wires bundled in a plastic sheath. Since every station used that kind of wiring. It's a mystery to me how engineers could recognize their own wires.

"Snip!"

Roy and Jim went on cutting. Several seconds passed, suddenly the door of Channel 5's remote truck flew open and out came a couple of engineers. They were swearing and yelling something to the effect their program had just died. In broadcaster talk, that meant they were no longer on the air. They were irate!

Seeing the commotion, Roy and Jim stopped cutting and snipping for a moment, looked at each other and shrugged.

"Noooo!" They said in unison, then looked around to see if anyone else was cutting and snipping. The answer was no.

"Damn it!" Roy said.

"Let's give 'em a hand," Jim said. "That way they'll think it was someone else and not us!"

Regardless of the circumstances, the unwritten code of the engineers has been to help out the other guy. It's not very competitive, but it was the nature of the people who worked in the business then.

Roy and Jim eventually 'fessed up and apologized. Channel 5 let them sweat a little, then accepted the apology.

Engineer Roy Sillence in the KOMO-TV tape room several years after the cable cutting incident in which KING-TV's Republican convention coverage was "cut" short. Roy said he was sorry...but notice the smile.

CHAPTER 13

" The Name of the Game Is......."

"I can't wait until I graduate and get into this business." the young man in the front seat said. His eyes were wide with wonder and there was an urgency in his voice. "I'm really looking forward to doing this for real!"

At the wheel of the KOMO-TV news car was Cameraman Bob Turner, Reporter John Sandifer was in the back and they were headed for Yakima, via Snoqualmie Pass. It wasn't unusual to have a "civilian" along on a news story. KOMO-TV, to its credit, seemed to go out of the way to help young students prepare for a career in broadcast journalism. Often that meant allowing University of Washington Communications students to spend a day "in-the-field" with a news team. The student was usually paired with a "seasoned" television news veteran. So when this wide-eyed, rather portly student showed up at the assignment desk one morning, the most available "seasoned" veteran was John Sandifer. The Kid, as Sandifer called him, was naive and bore an expression of wonderment as he surveyed the busy news room around him. Seasoned Sandifer, a serious-minded journalist who could make the simplest stories into scandalous intrigues, was a sharp contrast to The Kid.

On this particular day, Seasoned Sandifer, The Kid and Cameraman Turner were headed to Eastern Washington to do a story about the apple harvest... hardly the stuff of Watergate. But if there was something out of the ordinary in the orchards, John would find it. Because the trip was about three hours, Sandifer began to ask questions of the young man to pass the time. It didn't take long for the conversation to get around to what The Kid wanted out of his career.

"When I get into the business," the young man told John, "I'm going to call myself Wayne Shannon!"

John smiled. "What?" he asked.

"Wayne Shannon," came the reply, "I'm going to be known as Wayne Shannon. That's what I want to be called when I get on the air!"

Sandifer smiled as he rolled his eyes. *Oh brother*, he sighed to himself, then asked, "What's wrong with your own name, kid?

Before the young man could answer, John added, "Ya know, Kid, we're in a business that depends on truth. That's our goal, the truth." He continued, "Think about it, how could we face an audience night after night, trying our best to tell the truth about world events and make people believe it, if we aren't even using our own names?"

It was another question, but John didn't wait for an answer.

"We've got a lot of that now....er, I mean look around. Everywhere you go there are 'Bobby Holidays' and 'Jimmy Sundays'....Geeez," Sandifer said, "everybody and his brother wants to use a fancy name."

Seasoned Sandifer was just getting warmed up. He continued...

"Ya know there's nothing wrong with using your own name. I did, er, still do and I'm damn proud of it. You should be, too!"

It was the end of the speech. The kid looked as if he were in shock. Sandifer, content that he had made his point, looked The Kid straight in the eye and said; "By the way Kid, what is your real name?"

After a slight pause, The Kid blurted out, "My name is Wayne Schitzel!"[6]

The remainder of the trip was made in silence.

---

[6] It must be said that the Schitzel family name is, in fact, an honorable one and Wayne might have kept it had he been in another profession. The business of television news reporting is, however, one in which names of unusual pronunciation do not abound, for obvious reasons.

CHAPTER 14

The Great White...Hoax!

Back in television's black and white days there was a cops and robbers program on the air entitled "The Naked City." It was characterized by its opening line which said in effect, "There are eight million stories in the Naked City...." The Naked City was, of course, New York, but the fact is there are millions of stories in any city and it's up to guys like me to find them. Often that means some good hard digging while at other times they fall into your lap like so much jello sliding off a paper plate. And what makes a better-than-average reporter is the ability to recognize a story when it does slide off the paper plate.

I have in my career tried to counsel young reporters if someone calls in with a story or what they think is a story...CHECK IT OUT! All you have to lose is some time, and if the story is a winner, then take a bow.

In 1968, while working the night shift, I received a call from a fisherman who was on his way back to Seattle from somewhere in the Pacific Ocean. He was calling from the ship's radio and he explained that he was due to arrive at Pier 58 around midnight and I should be there to meet him.

"Why?" I asked.

He wouldn't tell me over the radio, but insisted that I should be there and bring a cameraman. It would be worth my while, he promised. I asked if he had called anyone else and he said he hadn't. I explained to him that I was reluctant to request a "shooter" to work beyond his normal shift, especially on the word of someone I didn't even know. He insisted.

My journalistic instincts told me it could be a great story, although it may have been wishful thinking. As I had told countless others...all I had to lose was time. The difficulty, of course, is that you are relying on someone else's news judgment. What is news to one person isn't necessarily news to another and the ultimate judgment is the reporters. Therefore he or she must check it out.

After promising dinner, a note to his Mom and my firstborn, Cameraman Steve Ramaley agreed to go with me. We arrived at the pier at the stroke of midnight to find a crowd of people jammed around the small purse seiner that was bobbing up and down alongside. I didn't see any other news cars around. Ok, I thought to myself....if it is a story, we have it alone!

No reporter wants or tries to look like an idiot, or like one of those reporters characterized on TV shows as a pushy-get-the-story-at-any-cost type. Caution. Be cool, I thought, just saunter up to the boat like one of the curious on-lookers, but don't tip your hand. These thoughts went through my mind as I got out of the car. No way did I want this to turn out to be nothing and look like a fool trying to cover it.

I suggested the cameraman leave his gear in the car until we had a chance to check it out. He did and we walked cautiously over to the edge of the pier. Just as we got there some joker yelled.

"Hey you guys, where's your camera?"

Wonderful. I smiled. Then we saw it. There in the back of the fishing boat, its tail sticking several feet out over the fantail was the biggest shark I have or no doubt will ever see. It was chalky gray in color with a mouth the size of an open fifty gallon oil drum. Blood oozed from the mouth.

Suddenly any doubts about this being a story disappeared. We went to work.

The shark, according to the captain of the fishing boat, had become entangled in seines somewhere off the coast of Washington.

Later we determined that it was in fact a great white, a species more likely found in the Southern Hemisphere than in the colder waters of the North Pacific.

Needless to say it was our lead story the next evening, and it was exclusive. And all it cost was about an hour and a half of our time. So the next time some jello falls into your lap...check it out!

CHAPTER 15

The Ears Have Walls

"Hello, Senator Jackson's Office."

"Is the Senator there?" I asked

"Who may I say is calling?" the receptionist answered back.

"Bill Brubaker," I said, "KOMO in Seattle."

"Just a moment."

I tried to figure out just how long it would take her to either buzz the Senator or get back to me herself. I wasn't too far off, because about the time I figured it out, the Senator was on the line.

I couldn't help but wonder if non-media persons could reach a United States Senator as easily. It wasn't uncommon for someone in my business to call Senator Jackson or any other lawmaker for that matter...it was part of the news gathering business. And it was standard procedure to inform the Senator that it was a news call and you would like to turn on a tape recorder with which to record the conversation. It was very important that, if the conversation was to be played on the air, there be no noise or interference with the quality of the recording. This was the early

1960s and there were no electronic or mechanical devices to protect the quality...about the surest way to take care of any problem was to cup your hand over the phone while the Senator talked and hoped he did likewise when you talked.

So there we were, the Senator and me, conducting a routine interview when all of a sudden came the rasping-razor blade-down-the-blackboard voice of Annabelle.

"Are you through?" the voice barked.

"What was that?" The Senator asked.

"That," I replied, "was Annabelle, the KOMO switchboard operator."

"What is an Annabelle?" The Senator can ask good questions as well as answer them, I thought to myself.

It's not as if this sort of thing hadn't happened before, but it was the first time it happened to me. The news director told me there would be days like this and frankly I was aggravated, after all I was talking to a United States Senator. That little fact however didn't phase Annabelle one bit. Senator or not, she needed that line and was going to get it. No big shot Senator was about to filibuster her switchboard.

When I began to work at KOMO Radio, Annabelle was already legendary. She was small, grey of hair and definitely her own person. I could not understand how she managed to keep her job. It wasn't her phone-side manner, that's for sure. Busting in on conversations was her way of letting you know who was in charge. And no matter how loudly one complained, the behavior was casually brushed aside with "...That's Annabelle!" It was also clear that no green-behind-the-ears-just hired reporter was going to change that.

So you lived with it...and spent a great deal of time trying to avoid Annabelle's proclivity for "joining in," or devising ways to trap her. Not that it would change anything mind you, but it just might keep Annabelle off your phone and on someone else's.

One of the more devious ploys to "get" Annabelle was a faked affair-by-phone between one of the reporters and the news room secretary. Each day they would call one another from an outside phone so that the conversation was sure to go through the switchboard. In a typical conversation the pair would exchange pleasantries and then make plans to meet somewhere in the building. It was great fun, since the entire news room knew that Annabelle was listening to every word.

The idea was that Annabelle would tell someone upstairs of the illicit affair and when exposed, the ploy would in turn expose her and the problem would be solved. Did it work? Of course not! It only served to entertain her and the only result really was that she looked at the news room secretary and the reporter differently.

Not long after that incident however, Annabelle finally got hers. When a reporter was out in the field, standard procedure called for him or her to phone in their stories, have them taped, then move on to the next one. One particular day, the News Director himself was in the field and following his own established procedure, phoned in his reports. I was on the other end of the line when he phoned. My routine, after having been Annabelled, was to warn the caller, boss or not, to be careful, that Annabelle might be listening.

"I am not!" came the rasping-razor blade-down-the-blackboard voice. It was followed by a short gasp. Suddenly Annabelle, after years of stealth, had been discovered. And it was on tape. The News Director and I could hardly contain ourselves.

Within weeks Annabelle was gone. I like to think it was because we in the news room were so clever. The truth of the matter was Annabele retired...gone forever to a place no doubt where the lines weren't so busy.

CHAPTER 16

Perfect Pitch

One of my all time favorite characters in television was Dick Guthrie who had the deepest most resonant voice I ever heard. His booming voice belied his size. My guess was that he weighed no more than 100 pounds wringing wet. For that reason he was never seen on the tube, but instead heard doing the station breaks between programs and commercials. He also was responsible for reading the news when the station signed off the air each night.

Dick was a fussy sort, making sure each and every word was pronounced as the NBC Handbook of Pronunciation had intended them to be and his copy, whether it was a commercial or news, had to be edited just so! Dick was a font of knowledge and knew everything, too. And if he didn't know he had an opinion and was never shy in letting his colleagues at the station know it.

One such opinion was that he had perfect pitch. That is he could, by his own ear, determine the frequency and quality of any tone on the musical scale. "Prove it!" we would demand. But since none of us in the studio crew (I was working as a floor director then) had perfect pitch his attempts to prove it were not convincing.

Dick did not like to be doubted, so while his "perfect pitch" was the subject of kidding, it was Dick's hot button and the mere mention of it could spark an exchange.

The debate raged. Did he or didn't he have perfect pitch? It needed to be settled.

One of Dick's duties was to prepare and read the news when the station signed off the air. Often he would be in the news room ripping copy off the news wire machines and pasting it together to make a news-cast. Other times he would ask the reporters in the radio or television news departments to save their last newscast for him to read on the air. Whatever approach he took he did so with characteristic care and detail.

In true conspiratorial fashion the studio crew and I agreed that it was time to end the perfect pitch controversy once and for all and we would do it with one of Dick's own newscasts. We would fabricate a news story that would somehow refute Dick's claim and "slip" it in his copy when he wasn't looking. That way, we thought, not only would he get the message, he would read it on the air. Timing had to be just right however, since fussy old Dick would no doubt read and re-read his copy several times before going on the air with it.

My job in this particular exercise was to prepare the copy. It had to look just like it came off the news wire and be written in a style that would leave no doubt to the reader or the listener that it was the real thing. That meant the story could not be typed on a regular news room typewriter, but on the same machine that types news wire copy.

I enlisted the help of Marty Herwald who was the Seattle Bureau Chief for United Press International who let me use one of the bureau's teletype writers.

Acoustical scientists at California's Livermore Laboratories have discovered a rare breed of dog they claim solves once and for all the mystery of perfect pitch. Until now, the scientists say, no mammal had ever been found that could respond to the exact frequency of tones on the musical scale.

The dog, a small African Mongrel, is the pet of a family that lived near Doctor Hirum Foster, one of the acoustical scientists working on the project. Doctor Foster told UPI that he often worked on the project at home and discovered one day the neighbor's dog was barking as he worked. "I then discovered," Foster stated, "the dog only barked when I hit what I believed to be a perfect pitch tone!"

Doctor Foster said they have further tests to conduct, but that early observations indicate that the "perfect pitch" myth is no longer a myth.

"Until now," he said, "no mammals, not even humans were believed to have perfect pitch." He added, "There is still no evidence that humans possess this quality."

-30-

That done, the next obstacle was to get the story into Dick's news copy. A diversion, that's it! A diversion, we'll get someone to get Dick's attention just before he goes on the air and one of us will slip the story into the stack of wire copy Dick had assembled for the news.

Dick may have been fussy and somewhat aggravating with his know-everything attitude, but he was also very bright.

We waited that night to hear "our" story on the news, wondering what Dick would do when he read it. We waited...and nothing! He didn't read it. Did he even see it? Probably, but we'll never know for sure. Our guess was that he made one last pass though the copy, recognized something he hadn't read before and tossed it just to be safe. Whatever the explanation from that moment on, Dick never again mentioned perfect pitch...and we never asked.

CHAPTER 17

The Burrito Express

Winning an "Emmy" was just about the most exciting thing to happen to me in my thirty-year broadcasting career. "Emmy," an eleven-inch high gold statuette, is given by the National Academy of Television Arts and Sciences for outstanding performance in a variety of endeavors. And it makes little difference if the award is presented by the National Chapter of the Academy of Television Arts and Sciences or a local chapter. It is a high honor and the highlight of one's career.

In most cases, Emmys are presented for demonstrating a quality of craftsmanship that is far above the daily norm. Awards in the broadcast news business are most often given for Best Spot News Coverage, News Documentary, Best Coverage of a Continuing Event and so on. In my case however, it was none of these. In fact the story for which I was awarded this coveted prize would have gotten no more than thirty seconds of air time had it not been for the prolific camera work of Dave Mann and News Producer Dean Bunting, who succumbed to the argument that there was more to a routine accident than met the eye.

"And the winner is......'The Burrito Express;' KOMO-TV; Bill Brubaker, Producer; Dave Mann Cameraman!"

"Thank you, Ladies and Gentlemen," I said at the podium, afraid my voice would crack. "I am honored. I wish to thank KOMO for giving me this chance; Washington State University for educating me; my wife, Marlene; my children; Cameraman Dave Mann; News Producer Dean Bunting and Tom Richardson!"

Tom Richardson was a long-haul trucker from Texas, somewhere around El Paso as I recall. Even as a trucker with lots of miles logged he had never been to Washington State. This was his first look at Seattle, too, so it wasn't unexpected that he might find himself heading up the steep Queen Anne Hill Counterbalance in his semi-tractor and forty-foot trailer full of frozen burritos. One can only wonder where he got his directions since his destination was a food storage facility on Harbor Island...miles away in the opposite direction.

As he he rounded the next-to-the-last hill on the Counterbalance, Tom doubled-clutched his rig to a lower gear and headed up the last short, steep pitch to the top. Then with a shudder and loud crunch the Peterbilt's driveshaft twisted like a soft pretzel and fell to the pavement below. Before Tom knew what was happening the giant rig began rolling backwards down the Counterbalance...a straight shot toward Elliott Bay. He jammed on the brakes, set the emergency and waited, not yet knowing what had gone wrong, and he wasn't about to get out to take a look.

KOMO Television news had just made the transition from news film to video tape, a process dubbed "ENG" for electronic news gathering. It was not an easy change for the "shooters." The equipment was far more bulky, ultimately requiring a second person to handle the recording equipment. And the cameraman's "eye" was in most cases replaced by the automatic iris, which regulated the exposure. The more positive aspect of ENG, however, was the ability to shoot lots of material without having to worry about the cost of film and its processing. Editors usually had lots of material from which to make their stories...that is if they had time to go through it all.

In the case of Tom Richardson's Burrito Express, the unlimited ability to shoot lots of pictures paid off in a big way.

Cameraman Dave Mann was sent to the Counterbalance after hearing of the mishap on the police radio. Frankly, visions of this eighteen wheeler caroming off into Elliott Bay was enough to get the most skeptical of newsies off and running. When Dave arrived, Tom was sitting in the cab of the express smoking a cigarette and making sure the brakes held. He had been doing that for about twenty minutes. Within minutes, a giant wrecker arrived, a diesel powered cab-over affectionally called the "Green Monster" by its owners, City Towing, which specialized in heavy rescues. As Dave shot through his first roll of video tape, the Green Monster hooked up and began to pull the Burrito Express over that last pitch to a side street.

Nothing! The Express wouldn't budge. At best the whole tractor trailer would bounce up and down a bit, but couldn't be coaxed the fifty feet to safety. Clearly, the Green Monster wasn't enough. Enter the "Green Dragon," a slightly larger diesel powered wrecker. If the Green Dragon couldn't do it...well, the "Express" was destined to end up in Puget Sound.

By now a large crowd lined both sides of the "balance" and cheered Tom Richardson as if he were some sort of folk hero, which if he ever took his foot off the brake he would certainly be...the stuff of which songs are sung and legends are made. In a matter of moments the huge wreckers had rescued the "express" and its stressed-out driver, and cameraman Dave Mann was headed back to the station.

"Give me thirty seconds," the News Producer Bunting said, "and we'll have Brubaker write it!"

Dave had shot enough tape to create a feature-length movie so thirty seconds shouldn't have been a problem. Except it was great stuff. He had managed to capture a lot of emotion and drama. It occurred to both of us that this "thirty seconds" could make a terrific feature piece. I told Dave to edit the piece to tell the story and I would sell it to the producer.

"You want what?" Dean asked.

"Three minutes," I said, "This is great stuff and we have a wonderful story."

Now a television news producer has a difficult job at best, trying to shape an hour-long news program and balance the various stories that compete for the limited time. Accidents don't usually get a lot of attention from producers or reporters. This one did happily and the three-minute piece was an immediate hit.

But never in a million years would any of us have dreamed that a chain-smoking truck driver and sixteen tons of burritos would make for an Emmy! Thanks, Tom!

CHAPTER 18

Blas Pasis is Dead,
Long Live Blas Pasis

Usually a call to John Sandifer meant a tip on the latest goings on in Seattle's underworld or someone wanted him to investigate a misdeed of one sort or another. But this call wasn't from some First Avenue snitch, but a young couple in Bellevue who wanted to help a friend. Usually a call of this kind would go to the consumer affairs reporter...if we had one. We didn't! Or to the action line editor...if we had one. We didn't have one of those either. Or it might have gone to the assignment desk for assignment to any one of a dozen field reporters on the staff. But the call went to John, personally. A serious man, John was never one to turn down a plea for help...especially if he smelled a story in it.

The request in this case was on behalf of a seventy-three year old Filipino man who wanted more than anything on earth to be an American Citizen. Normally not a problem given time, but Blas Pasis didn't have much time...he was dying of cancer. The friends of the old man explained that Blas Pasis had come to America in the thirties, became a successful

79

truck farmer in the Kent Valley and suddenly a lifetime had passed. After a recurring illness had been diagnosed as cancer, becoming an American citizen was suddenly important to Blas Pasis as he faced the inevitable.

John went to work.

He told the viewers in the first of several reports that Blas had tried and failed several times to become a citizen. Part of the problem, Sandifer reported, was Blas's health, but he also choked up when taking the citizenship test. His mind went blank and the harder he tried the more this prize eluded him.

Following the first report, John enlisted the help of immigration lawyer Dan Danilov. He was also touched by the old man's story and together they marched Blas to the immigration office for another try. But sadly, the attempt ended like those before it. Tired and sick, Blas failed the test. That night on the evening news Sandifer told his audience what had happened.

After work, instead of going home, John went over to Blas' house where he spent the entire night preparing the old man for the test. Hour after hour he drilled Blas on questions about the government. What kind do we have? What are its branches? And so on until John was convinced the old man knew the answers.

But knowing the answers wasn't enough. Even if Blas did pass the citizenship test, it could take days, perhaps weeks before he could become a citizen. And with cancer eating away at his life, it was a race against time, a race Blas Pasis could easily lose.

Among those following the story and Sandifer's daily television news reports was James Turnage, Northwest Region Director of the U.S Immigration Service. Like most of us, Turnage was touched. He informed Sandifer and Danilov that he would do everything in his power to waive certain technical requirements when and if Blas passed the test.

Once again Blas, John and attorney Danilov marched to the now all-too-familiar Immigration Office to re-take the test. This was it...Sandifer had coached him...the Immigration Service said it would waive the time requirements...it was now up to Blas. As the old man wrestled with the questions, Sandifer and Danilov paced outside the testing room like expectant fathers. They waited...and waited.

"I wonder if it's like a jury trial?" Sandifer questioned, "I mean the longer it takes the better the chance of a verdict in our favor."

"It doesn't always work that way," Danilov replied.

In what seemed like an entire day, but was a little over an hour, Blas emerged from the testing room. He was tired and the strain showed on his frail body. But the grin....a grin that exposed a million teeth... told his two companions all they needed to know.

Sandifer and Danilov grabbed their prize student and after appropriate hugs and pats on the back, raced to the U.S. District Court in a flurry of umbrellas and raincoats. There, as John and Dan watched Blas's dream-come-true, he became a citizen of the United States of America. They had done, in a day, what normally takes a month or more. And with tears streaming down his face this frail seventy-three year-old man clutched his citizenship papers to his heart.

Blas Pasis is dead now. But before he died, not long after he became a citizen, he visited the KOMO-TV news room. Clutching the arm of his friend John Sandifer, Blas slowly walked to each person there and shook hands. "I am a citizen," he would say and he smiled.

Then he turned before he left and said to the assembled reporters and cameramen, "Do you know what I did today?" Then without waiting for an answer, he declared, "I registered to vote...I am going to vote before I die!"

Reporter Don McGaffin with Richard Nixon, who was campaigning for the presidency when this spirited interview took place in the KOMO-TV studios in 1968. Security was so tight that when Author Bill Brubaker tried to get into the adjacent studio to do the evening news, Secret Service Agents wouldn't let him in. They relented, however, when Brubaker handed the agent the script and suggested he read the news.

CHAPTER 19

"I'll Be Back in a Moment...a Moment!"

The director of a television news program usually has but three choices as he directs a program. One, he can keep his eyes glued on wall monitors in the control booth with an occasonal glance at the script or....two, keep his eyes glued to the script with an occasional glance at the monitors or...three, do both, which is what he or she is supposed to do. It happens to be the best way, too!

You meet all types of directors in a lifetime of television news and most fall into category number three. However, I can recall an incident with a category two type director who couldn't even manage an occasional glance at the monitors. Most of the time this type of director can get away with burying himself in the script and call the shots...but this time, he didn't.

It is important to know that the assembly of a television news program is not a haphazard activity. It is a carefully planned process whereby stories are covered, taped and edited. And scripts are written and given to the newscaster and the director, identical scripts telling them what is to be said and what is to appear on the television screen. If it's going well, the newscaster reads and the director follows along and does what the script says. The danger is, of course, that should the wrong video appear on a monitor, everyone but the director, who's the only one who could do anything about it, will know.

In this particular incident, our newscaster, a former newspaper man from the Bay Area named Don McGaffin, was well into his newscast and our category two type director was well buried into the script, totally oblivious to what was on the control room monitors. Part one of the newscast ended with, "...We'll be back with more news in a moment!" There was a slight pause, and a fade to black and then the commercial. So far so good! The newscaster gently tapped his pencil. He had about a minute.

Meanwhile back in the booth, the director, nose buried in the script, waited for the cue that would signal him into action once again. Thirty seconds... forty-five...almost there.

Down on the studio floor our waiting newscaster accidentally flipped his pencil onto the floor. All newscasters carry pencils you know...sort of a designation of office. The pencil dropped to the floor next to the podium behind which McGaffin stood. In television, they say, timing is everything. I still don't now who "they" are, but "they" are right. Just as McGaffin bent down to retrieve the pencil, the director snapped, "Take camera one!" His head planted firmly in the script, the director instantly responded to the last words of the commercial. Had he been looking at his monitor, he would have noticed there was no one there....

Live, before all was an empty set. There was a podium....a curtain, and no newscaster! He was on his hands and knees behind the podium, looking for the pencil. When the director realized what had happened he did the only thing he knew...he panicked!

While the director was having a fit in the control booth, McGaffin, still on his hands and knees, realized what had happened. "Do I," he questioned, "stand up and try not to look like a jack-in-the-box, or do I crawl out of here and try to re-group?" Time was passing. So was the audience.

During what seemed like nothing short of a lifetime, McGaffin crawled out of the studio on his hands and knees and out of sight of the camera, hoping beyond hope the director wouldn't do anything dumb, like take his picture. Off camera, he adjusted his tie and walked calmly, if not briskly, back to the podium. He resumed his newscast where he left off, never once acknowledging that for the past thirty to forty seconds the audience, what remained of it, had been looking at an empty set.

As for the director....last thing I knew, he was still looking at the script.

CHAPTER 20

Gin!

Television anchors are not as a rule superstitious, that is, they don't usually carry rabbit's feet or wear a "lucky" tie or scarf. But like most performers who appear before a camera or live audience they indulge in a certain amount of ritualistic behavior. I once had a co-anchor who wouldn't talk before going on the air but fell into a sort of trance. There was another who continually cleared his throat. It was a wonder he had any voice left by the time we went on the air.

In my case, insisting that two glasses of water be placed next to my chair on the set for each newscast was as much pragmatic as ritualistic. The large studio color-cameras used in the sixties needed a lot of light in order to capture a clear image...about twice as much light as required by the more modern equipment of today. Twice as much light meant twice as much heat and often the studio temperature would reach the 90s. So to avoid dehydration during an hour-long news program I drank a lot of water.

In what became a ritual I would ask for two glasses of water, drink one just before air time and then sip the other throughout the program. It was always the same; rush into the studio from the news room, put the microphone on, get some last minute makeup, settle in the chair, arrange my copy and gulp down the first glass of water. And that's the way it was, day after day after day...that is until one day in the summer of 1967.

There was nothing remarkable about the day or the news for that matter. I had completed all the final edits and headed to the studio, a tad bit late as usual. The floor director helped me with the microphone, dabbed some Tan Number 2 makeup on my forehead and yelled to the rest of the studio crew to "Stand by!" (We were about a minute from air time) "My water! where's my water?" I muttered. There on the table next to me were two glasses of water. I grabbed one and gulped it down as fast as I could.

"Thirty seconds," the floor director barked.

I glanced at the clock, but I couldn't see it. My eyes were watering, I began to sweat and I could barely speak. I gasped for air. "Go to commercial" I whispered as I realized that the water I had hurriedly swallowed wasn't water.

It looked like water and it smelled like water, but it wasn't water. It was gin! The floor directors had substituted my two glasses of water with two glasses of gin and counted on my ritualistic behavior to carry the prank off.

We used every commercial in the news program before I regained enough composure to continue. In those days I was anchoring the news by myself and there was no co-anchor who could help me out.

As for the glasses of water, I still insisted on two thereafter, but from that point on instead of gulping one and nursing the other, I decided that the wiser course was to sip them both.

The "barge" from which all stations including
KOMO-TV broadcast the hydroplane races.
It was sturdier than it looked.

CHAPTER 21

Stan Sayres is the Pits!

From the 1950s on, one of the things you could be sure the Seattle television industry would do, besides News, Sports and Weather, was the annual summer madness known as the "Hydroplane Races." It was the ultimate in station to station rivalry, with all three and sometimes four stations doing exactly the same thing. Like clockwork, the city's three major television stations filed into the Stan Sayres Pits the first week of August each summer. It was a move that would make a logistician proud, tons of equipment followed by engineers, technicians, announcers and a number of people whose assigned tasks mystified me, but wore the proper badges. If they did nothing, and some did nothing, they had a view of the race unobstructed by the thousands of fans lining the shores of Lake Washington.

Coverage of Seafair's hydro-mania was as much a showcase for the latest broadcast equipment as it was entertainment for the viewer. It was sort of a media trade show where one station would show up with the longest remote trailer...another the longest lens and yet another the newest mini-camera that could be taped to a driver's helmet. It also provided a great testing ground, because if it worked at the "races" it would surely work back in the studio.

The hydroplane race, which many times involved just about everybody in the station, gave technical staff a chance to get out of the studio...it gave the production staff an opportunity to try out new equipment and escape the restrictions that studio television placed on their skills...And for the announcing staff...well for Sports Director Bruce King it was still sports, but it allowed the rest of us to share some of the glory of the sports world...you know the thrill of victory, that sort of stuff. I'm sure Mister KOMO knew that and was willing to go to the trouble and expense to give his employees the opportunity to exercise their creative urges. KOMO was like that!

In 1974 Seattle Seafair officials elected to charge an admission fee for the first time. It turned out to be the last time, too. The former Naval Air Station at Sand Point was the chosen site. Until now the three hundred thousand people who attended the races were able to sit along the shores of Seward Park, on the grass and in the shade. Now for an admission, they were going to be able to watch the race from a dirt bank with no shade. It was a lot to ask.

It was a new experience for us as well. The once familiar course bounded by Seward Park and the Lacy Murrow Bridge wasn't there. And the barge from which we broadcast was no barge at all, but scaffolding on scaffolding constructed on shore. It looked more like the bridge on the River Kwai than anything else. And the Stan Sayres Pits, which were permanent and designed just for the hydroplane races, were replaced by Bailey bridges to nowhere.

But the unfamiliar surroundings were offset somewhat by innovations that promised to make for an exciting five hours of racing. Most prominent was Hydroplane Racing's first jet-powered boat, the U-95, and between heats the Navy's Blue Angels were scheduled to perform.

Racing was scheduled to get underway precisely at noon, following a drivers' meeting and some tense-up time. For the broadcast crews, like the mechanics working on the boats, the day began at dawn with last minute checks. Bruce King and I arrived about seven in the morning, as I recall. There wasn't a great deal to do, however, since we had been covering the time trials all week and our homework was finished. We knew who was driving what, how fast, to where and why. Our remaining task was to outline the broadcast schedule with the production and engineering staffs and to touch base with the pit reporters who this day were Harry Sloan, Joe Washington and Ruth Walsh.

The task of the "pit reporter" was to seek out the winners and the losers after each race and ask them why...and if they cared. Believe it or not there was always some guy who didn't care if he won or lost, but how he drove the game. Sometimes getting a winner or a loser without falling off the finger pier or stepping on someone's hydroplane, which was a definite no-no, was not so easy when you considered that there were six or seven other reporters trying to do the same. The pit reporters were instructed to keep their reports short, to the point and better than the other guy's report, then cue back to the announcers with, "...Back to you on the barge!"

It was decided to say barge, since that's what we had been saying for years. Besides "...Back to you on the scaffold!" didn't sound right.

Pit reporters, when not interviewing winners or losers or watching specific boats, were pretty much left to their own devices to find interesting and visually stimulating stories. While Harry and Joe divided the boats between them, Ruth was assigned general interest stuff, people stories that could be used between heats. Bruce, of course, did the play-by-play or lap-by-lap descriptions of the race and I did the color, which meant I occasionally interjected with a "That's right, Bruce!" or "...He's really driving well, Bruce." (Go ahead and laugh, I had a great view of the race and I didn't have to pay!)

Another phenomenona of the I-can-do-anything-you-can-do-better world of hydroplane broadcasting was the guest expert. You probably thought the expert commentator was a more recent innovation of football and baseball. No way, hydroplane racing had been using "expert" commentators as far back as the forties and fifties when Slo Mo was really "slo." However, as in modern times, expert commentators employed by the hydro broadcasts were non-broadcasters who knew more than anyone about the sport because they were or once were participants.

KING-TV, who many believe invented hydroplane racing so they could broadcast it, had as their expert commentator Bill Muncy, a national champion many times over who counted among his accomplishments the sinking of a Coast Guard Cutter in 1955—which he knifed like soft butter with an errant hydroplane.

Hard to beat that! We tried, though, by also enlisting the services of a hydroplane driver. He was young, handsome, articulate and the current driver of the U-95, the world's first jet-powered unlimited hydroplane. What a team, Bruce, Me, Harry, Joe, Ruth and driver Leif Borgeson.

It was time.

As a chilly north wind blew across the lake creating just the right amount of ripple for the hydros, the boats made their way onto the course. Heats 1-A and 1-B went off without a hitch. So far the program was great. Heat 1-C was next. It was the race everyone was waiting for, the one in which the fastest and biggest boats would compete including the jet-powered U-95. We would have to do without the services of Leif since he would be driving in this race.

First lap, the crowd was on its feet as the giant turbine-powered hydro entered the third turn. Suddenly an explosion occurred, barely heard over the deafening noise of hydro engines. A red flare shot skyward and the boats scattered and stopped. We looked but could not see the U-95. Was Leif okay? We didn't know. We did know, however, that Hydro Racing's first jet-powered boat was on the bottom of Lake Washington. It was also clear that Leif wasn't going to be back on the announcing stand for a while, if at all. We weren't going anywhere. Bruce, Harry, Joe, Ruth and I would have to vamp until the restart of Heat 1-C. No sweat!

Around the horn...first to Harry who did a reaction piece with the crew of the U-95...."That's it from here," Harry said, "now let's go to George Washington..." George? Gads Harry, his name is Joe. From Geor...er Joe, we tossed to Ruth who was up to her curls in people trying to get some comments on what they saw, then it was back to Bruce on the "barge."

Now if everything went as planned, the pit reports were timed to coincide with the resumption of the race so when it was tossed back to the barge, the boats were about to enter the course. However, if you couldn't "time" the pit reports for whatever reason or there were unexpected delays, then the studio could roll any one of a dozen or so feature reports taped earlier for just such delays...features like hydro button

95

trading, what drivers did in the off-season and so on. While each reporter did several of these "features," there was rarely enough time to use them all.

Following the commercial break, we were ready to restart Heat 1-C. The boats were on the course, all except the turbine-powered U-95 which was on the bottom of the lake. Leif was all right, cooling his heels in a local hospital, for observation. He had been blown clear of the boat by the explosion, picked up by rescue helicopter and rushed to the hospital. The public address announcer blared the good news to the folks on shore and we did likewise to the people tuned in to our broadcast.

It was a good start and the thunderboats screamed by the barge and entered the South Turn. Everything looked good. Then the second turn...up the back stretch where the boats could reach speeds of 150 miles an hour or more. As they neared the North Turn, I heard Bruce yell to the audience that the Miss U-S had gone dead in the water. Once again red flares shot skyward as black smoke poured from the boat.

"There's smoke coming from the Miss U-S," Bruce said.

"That's right, Bruce," I added as we peered through binoculars to see if we could see the driver. We could and he appeared to be okay. He had apparently leaped over the side at the first sign of trouble.

Once again the flare in the air signaled to all that the race had been stopped.

As the remaining boats headed for the pits, our little band of reporters did likewise to get first hand reports of what had happened. Meanwhile back on the barge, Bruce and I "jes kep on talkin'." It took almost an hour to clear the lake of the burned-out hull of the Miss U-S and during that time we talked to about everyone we could and used up a couple of features as well. We had some more in the can in case Bruce and

I ran out of things to say. I might have, but Bruce could have talked for several days I'm sure...and never repeat himself.

The race officials had, by now, decided to run all the other heats while they worked out what to do with Heat 1-C. The remaining heats went off without incident and it was television coverage as usual....except it was getting very late in the day. Normally we would be wrapping up our coverage by now and heading for home.

While all this was going on, there was a very nervous Ruth Walsh pacing in the pits....not because this was her first hydro race. On the contrary, Ruth was the ultimate professional and any assignment handed her was done well. No, she was nervous because of dinner! Ruth, the benevolent Grande Dame of Seattle Broadcasting, was planning a gigantic spaghetti dinner for the entire Channel 4 broadcast crew. For almost a week her home had been transformed into a residential "old spaghetti factory" with pans of sauce as far as the eye could see and noodles hanging from every conceivable place. Ruth was nervous and she had a right to be. She had planned dinner for 6:30, give or take a half hour. Plenty of time, she reasoned, since the race would be over by 4:30. She looked at her watch...it was almost 6:30. Surely, she thought to herself, the people helping out back home would put everything on hold. After all the race was on hold, why not the spaghetti?

The seconds, minutes and hours ticked by and soon Bruce and I and the rest of the broadcast crew entered the "silly" phase of our broadcast. With little else to do but keep the program on the air, we began to tell and show our audience everything...well not everything! Before we signed off, the audience knew a whole lot more than they probably wanted to know about ducks, swimming, clouds and the color of every pleasure boat on Lake Washington. Youngsters passing by on waterskis became instant celebrities.

It was eight p.m. when word finally came that the re-run of Heat 1-C would take place. Oh joy, we thought, the end was in sight. Encouraged by the news, we psyched ourselves up for another try. Bruce set the stage again and recapped what had caused the long delay. I threw in a "That's right, Bruce" or two, then we tossed it around the horn. First to Harry, then to Joe and back to the barge.

"Let's find out what the crowd thinks of all this delay," Bruce announced. "Let's go to Ruth!"

"That's right, Bruce," I answered

Hearing her cue over an IFB, a device allowing her to hear the program and the director simultaneously, Ruth began frantically waving at the camera which was on a tower several hundred feet away and at least fifty feet high. She was trying to tell the director who was watching on his monitor that she wasn't ready. Too late.

"Take two," the director commanded.

It was immediately apparent to the audience that the cameraman wasn't ready either, because he produced a wide shot, so wide that it showed Ruth, standing all alone, barely visible, in a vacant field. No other living souls were around. While the broadcasters did their best to keep the folks at home entertained, those ever-so-important paying customers had gone home.

It was now up to Ruth, whose pasta dinner, like a number of the hydroplanes, didn't finish. She chuckled and explained to her audience, "Well...tee hee, everyone has gone home." Then she began to vamp, filling the time by talking about things as they came into her mind, but mostly paraphrasing comments made earlier by the fans who were no longer there.

While she described the desolate scene around her, her eye caught some movement....it was a man jogging through the field with his dog. Oh boy, Ruth thought, a real live person! So as the camera panned the giant vacant lot, Ruth eased over to the jogger and without the slightest loss of composure, began to interview him. She asked him how he liked the race.

"What race?" the man questioned, "I don't know about any race. I'm just out here to walk my dog and get some exercise."

A good time, Ruth thought, to toss it back to Bruce on the barge.

CHAPTER 22

You Have to Have Your Greens!

I wonder how Munji is getting along these days? Not that I miss him, you understand, it's just that...well, Munji was one of those delightful characters who come along too few times.

Munji was an Indian exchange student at the University of Washington where he was majoring in Communications. And as part of his studies he participated in the school's Internship Program. He wanted to be a news cameraman and was assigned to that task while at KOMO, but why and how he was assigned to the Sports Department remains a mystery.

He was a skinny kid with ebony black hair and flashing eyes, the whites of which contrasted with his dark skin. When armed with a forty-pound news camera, Munji was easy to find in a crowd.

One summer afternoon in the mid seventies, golf legend Sam Snead was in town as part of the annual Professional Golfers Tour whereby the "pros" played golf with the local professionals and celebrities, then conducted golf clinics which were usually open to the general public. Sam Snead was famous and just having him in town whether he picked up a golf club or not, was news...sports news. On this particular afternoon Snead was playing a round with the local pros at Seattle's Inglewood Country Club. Like most private clubs, Inglewood was well groomed and gave one the feeling of "posh" while passing through the gates and down the tree-lined drive to the beautiful old clubhouse.

Just as the folks who play there take their country club seriously, they take their golf seriously as well. One does not make noise when a golfer is putting... you replace your divots, if you have nerve enough to make a divot in the first place, and you don't sneeze during someone's backswing, especially when "Slammin'" Sammy Snead is on the course.

Since it was a sports story after all, the duty of covering the event fell to Harry Sloan. Harry had a great sense of humor. When doing his job, however, he demonstrated a certain intensity that could shut out all other things going on around him. The problem was that because he concentrated in the story, He tended to assume that his film crew, which today consisted of Munji, knew what they were doing and would operate with the same intensity.

Here's the situation. Snead, second to tee off, had slightly scooped his ball to the left of center fairway just short of the trees. He was about 100 yards from the green on the par four, 387-yard number one hole. As Snead and his partners proceeded down the fairway to where Snead's ball lay, the gallery, which was of considerable size as you might expect, moved with them. Snead had an easy pitch to the green.

Now Harry, eager to get the shot on film, urged Munji to do just that. Munji, as eager to please as Harry was eager to get the shot, scampered to the head of the gallery where, about ten yards away from the great golfer, he hoisted his camera to his shoulder and began to shoot. Snead, meanwhile, head bent over, was lining up the shot. He looked up and there directly between him and the green was Munji! Snead stopped, straightened up and lowered the golf club. Glaring at the skinny kid with the camera, Snead politely, but firmly told him to get the heck out of the way. Munji smiled, looked around to see if anyone noticed and got out of the way.

Harry, viewing all of this from the gallery cringed and hoped beyond hope that when he moved, Munji would not return to him, but just quietly step aside, film Snead and then go back to the station...alone.

No luck, Harry realized, as Munji jogged up to him with a "what did I do?" look on his face. This was not the time to explain, Harry thought and told Munji to get some pictures of Snead on the green.

"Okay Harry," Munji replied, in his clipped Indian accent, and off he ran. About halfway he screeched to a stop, wheeled around and ran back to where Harry was standing.

"Harry" he said, "Harry, old friend....what is a green?"

Munji didn't return for the next season of golf, oh not because he didn't know what a green was, or because he almost had a cavity filled by the great Sam Snead...no, Munji didn't return because he finished school and his internship and went on to "greener" fields. He now knows what a green is, but sadly, Slammin' Sammy Snead, will never really know what a Munji is!

Ray Ramsey

CHAPTER 23

When in Doubt
Do the Friendliest Thing!

A woman from Fort Lauderdale, Florida, whose name I cannot recall, described a weather forecaster thus:

> A weather forecaster is a person who passes as an exacting expert on the basis of being able to turn out with prolific fortitude an infinite series of maps and forecasts calculated from incomprehensible formulas with infinitesimal precision from vague assumptions based on debatable figures taken from alleged observations made with instruments of problematical accuracy by persons of dubious reliability and questionable mentality for the avowed purpose of amazing and confounding...laymen!

Sound like anybody you know?

Ray Ramsey, like me, was born and raised in Spokane, Washington. When he was born and raised in Spokane is a mystery. You see Ray has, over the years, closely guarded his age, not only by not telling anyone, but by his looks and lifestyle. About the only clue he's ever given me or the television audience was that his father worked for the Heinz Company, when Heinz had less than a dozen varieties. I can tell you, however, that one of the two things I remember most about being in the third grade is having tuna fish sandwiches and tomato soup when I came home from school for lunch. The other thing I remember vividly is a radio that played while I enjoyed my lunch...a program called KREM and Coffee Time hosted by a mile-a-minute talker by the name of Hayhead Ray. I was eight years old.

I had no idea that one day I would not only have the privilege of working alongside him, but that I would consider him a dear and devoted friend.

The road to fame and fortune as Channel 4's weatherman was as varied as the weather he forecast.

Telegrapher, mortician and ambulance driver were among the early professions earning him enough tuition to enter the Chouinard Art Institute in Los Angeles, California. It didn't last long, however. To hear him tell it, his brushes were too wide and his Glidden hat didn't fit. If his famed weather cartoon character Figus Theebee was the sum total of his training, then maybe there was another path to fame and fortune...acting maybe?

That didn't last much longer, but his stint at the famed Pasadena Playhouse allowed him opportunity to consort with the likes of Steve Allen and prepared him for his eventual role as a radio disk jockey. But just in case he couldn't be on the radio, Ray surmised that he might, with the proper training, be able to run one and off he scampered to Radio Engineering School. It must have seemed at the time a rather disorganized approach to a career, but looking back what better training to be a television weatherman than, a little art, a little acting and a little technical expertise?

106

With all that training, including a couple of college degrees, Ray joked his way into the good graces of Radio Pioneer Louis Wasmer and found a home in his hometown at KREM where in little or no time he had most of the city eating tuna sandwiches and tomato soup out of his hand. Even after successful careers on radio and television, this classic over-achiever completed a military career that saw him retire from the Air Force Reserve and for a decade or more he taught junior high school, a job few marines would even try in those days. That's all behind him now, he's through teaching and he's no longer playing with his omega blocks. He's retired, probably out to pasture...literally...playing with his beloved horses.

Our careers met in the mid sixties when "Hayhead" was hired by KOMO Television to be the station's weatherman. Those of us who knew Ray, either by reputation or personally, were delighted. It was in fact a bold step on the part of KOMO, which in those days was so conservative that it earned the nickname of "The Little Old Lady at Fourth and Denny." We all wondered just how the station was going to deal with flamboyant Ray, who for the past couple of years demonstrated on KOL Radio that he would do and say just about anything. The best way to describe Ray Ramsey was to use one of his own favorite words, anomaly, which means;

> The angular distance, as seen from the
> sun, of a planet from the point at which
> it is nearest to the sun.

In other words, "far out!" The word also means anything that deviates from the common rule...and that certainly fits Ray Ramsey.

There were other words that fit Ray Ramsey. In fact if Mister Webster didn't have one, Ray would make one up. The amazing thing was that the made up word usually worked. For example, one of Ray's favorite concoctions was *drismal*. It was a combination of the words dismal and drizzle which describes our Pacific Northwest weather to a tee. Now *drismal* weather can mean *slickery* conditions especially if there are *snifters* about. The word slickery comes from slick and slippery and when combined describe a condition that is slightly more than just slick or slippery. Contributing to this *slickery* condition can be a very light snowfall, sort of like sifted flour...*snifters*! The result of those conditions can and often is...*skittery*. Skidding of course makes up part of this word and skidding on snifters can make one jittery, even *skittery*.

Another way Ray often described our less-than-perfect conditions was by using the words *grody* and *snitzy*. It doesn't take much detective work to figure out that *grody* comes from the word gross, which means terrible and the word cruddy which also means terrible. It means a severe condition, which *snitzy* is, but not as bad as snitzy. The word is often used with *snifters* and means a light snowfall and possible *slickery* conditions. *Snitzy* conditions can be *nastiful*...*nastiful* describing the degree of *snitzy*.

On the other hand some weather is good and a *rejuberized* day can be *splendiferous*. In *rejuberized* we find the word rejuvenate, meaning of course to make new. The other word is exuberant which, when combined with rejuvenate means to make new with vigor. A *rejuberized* day is one in which the dawn comes up like thunder and a *splendiferous* day is just about the bluest skies you've ever seen.

Try this one: A *humungus* front, after *hunkering* off the coast has begun *sluggering* its way inland and is about to *splew* over the countryside. The word splew is not easy to define, even for Ray. Though more descriptive than definable, it is believed to be a combination of the words spray and threw, like *flang*...you know, fling, flang, flung is an action verb to describe movement. Slugger is to be sluggish, slow or plodding. Hunkering is no movement at all. Hunk refers to something very large and difficult to move. A large mass of clouds might be considered a hunk when it sits off the coast ready to pounce on unsuspecting picnickers...it is *hunkering*. And, of course, in order for that mass of clouds to *hunker* it must be *humungus*.[7]

And finally, there is, in the word world of Hayhead Ray, the word *labonza*. It is not, as some would have us believe an Italian dance or a Riviera dessert...it is that part of the human anatomy sometimes known as the fanny. One slips because of *nastiful, slickery snifters*, often falling on one's *labonza*.

But words alone did not a weatherman make. There were the weather forecasts themselves which were designed to dazzle if not confuse the viewer. A lot went into the preparation and presentation of one of Ray's weather reports, and it's the same today as it was in Ray's time.

Now the first thing Ray would say was *"The National Weather Service says...."* That was important, because the first rule of good weather forecasting was to immediately blame someone else for what he

---

[7] While editing this manuscript, Brian Herbert noted that he could not verify the spelling of "humungus." Of course you couldn't, Brian, it's a Ramsaying!

about to say. In his next line the weatherman would say, *"It was a beautiful day today in the Pacific Northwest..."* or, *"It was a wet day in the Pacific Northwest today."* The rule here was to say something with which most of the viewers would agree. *"The reason for such a (beautiful) (wet) (cloudy) day is a (high) (low) pressure system in the Gulf of Alaska."* But no self-respecting weather person would let that stand. Ray would then say, *"Some (bad) (good) (grody) weather is likely to spill over the ridge and change things."* He had now covered all the possibilities...and had a fifty-fifty chance of being right...or wrong.

Turning to the marine forecast, Ray would usually tell his audience that a *plethora* of fog and a *modicum* of wind were headed our way. The words plethora and modicum were designed to send the viewer madly dashing for the dictionary, while Ray then said anything he wanted.

Next came the immediate forecast. *"There will be fair skies through tomorrow with temperatures near sixty."* You'll notice he didn't say sixty-two or sixty-five. That way if the temperature reached forty-six, he figured that was close enough.

Now with all that said, Ray would then say something to the effect that the National Weather Service (displaced responsibility again) was always right, but that its timing was not always accurate. What he meant was that it could all change in a matter of hours...more like minutes, and that meant don't plan anything until you get up!

CHAPTER 24

Things That Go Bump in the Night

We've shared a lot, Bruce King, Ray Ramsey and me. In thirteen years of doing the the same show together there were problems; we shared those. There were days so boring you could fall asleep; we shared those. And there were moments of great hilarity; we shared those too. And the nature of television was, what we shared with each other, we often shared with you, the viewer.

One such "sharing" occurred in the mid seventies on News Final, KOMO's eleven o'clock news. I was anchoring, Bruce was handling the sports as usual and Ray had his hands full, literally, with two cuddly little dachshundt puppies. It seems the puppies needed attention and were left in the care of Hayhead for just that purpose. When it came time to go to work, Ray had little choice but to take the little critters along. So there we were in the studio, on the air, and as Ray began his weather report he saw fit to introduce his canine companions, then hand one to each of us. They were truly cute, small enough to fit in the palm of your hand and each with a red ribbon around its neck. It did little for the credibility of our news program, but as we were to learn later, the audience loved it.

Now you've no doubt noticed that often in television, especially news, the stations often try to "soften" the visual impact of going from news to a commercial, or back, with a picture of something. The picture can be a still scene or one in motion, or it can be a tease to the stories coming up. Its called a "bump" and usually works like this: The news person will say..."We'll be back with more news after this..." At that point the director calls for the commercial and while he and the audience wait the three to ten seconds for it to appear, he goes to the "bump." It's a good technique, easy to use and prevents any "dead-air"...those times when the screen is devoid of any picture.

By now you have no doubt figured out what the director figured out...the puppies would make a great "bump" to a commercial coming out of Ray's weather report. Bruce and I agreed and happily handed the cute little critters over to the floor manager. It was the floor manager's job to position the puppies so the studio camera could take their picture...for the "bump."

As Ray neared the end of his forecast, the floor manager aimed a studio spotlight on the studio floor and herded the puppies into the circle of light. The cameraman framed the picture. Anyone walking into the studio at that moment would have been set back by the sight of the camera tilted to the floor, Ray doing his weather, and the floor manager lying flat on his stomach trying to keep two cuddly little wiener dogs inside the circle of light.

Ray was getting closer to finishing.

The crew was tense...

The director was tense....

It was an exciting moment, actually...a "live" studio bump to the commercial.

It was time. A shiver of excitement swept over me as I said: "We'll be back with more news right after this!"

At that precise moment, the director in the booth called for the studio camera which was now trained on the two little dogs in the circle of light. It worked!

It was a wonderful moment. There live, in the studio, for all the world to see and in color, were two adorable little puppies, one climbing on the back of the other in the unmistakable act of mating.

I couldn't believe it. What incredible timing, I thought. I was stunned. Bruce was stunned and Ray, bless his heart, chuckled and mumbled something about how cute they were.

But from the director's booth, through a sixteen inch concrete wall and double panes of soundproof glass, the entire studio could hear, "OH GOD, NO!"

The crew was of absolutely no use, they were prostrate with laughter.

A "bump" usually takes no more that two or three seconds at most. That day it was two or three hours, at least.

KOMO-TV's grande dame, Ruth Walsh adjusts Bob Throndsen's tie as they prepare to do the evening news from the new "open" set. Breaking away from the "behind-the-desk" approach to television news was a bold step in 1978.